COLLECTED POEMS

1965-2018

COLLECTED POEMS
1965-2018

DAVID SUTTON

Greenwich Exchange

Greenwich Exchange, London

First published in Great Britain in 2019
All rights reserved

Printed and bound by imprintdigital.com
Cover design by December Publications
Tel: 07951511275

Greenwich Exchange Website: www.greenex.co.uk

Cataloguing in Publication Data is available
from the British Library

ISBN: 978-1-910996-23-2

for Gillian, with love and gratitude for sixty years

'I should use, as the trees and birds did,
A language not to be betrayed;
And what was hid should still be hid
Excepting from those like me made
Who answer when such whispers bid.'
    – Edward Thomas: 'I Never Saw That Land Before'

CONTENTS

from Out on a Limb (1969)

Out on a Limb *23*

Seaside Honeymoon *25*

Wedding Dress *27*

Division *27*

Two Trees *28*

The Tree of Frost *29*

The Flowers *30*

Stroke Case *31*

No Other Elegy *31*

The Ripples *32*

Summer Rain *33*

Lament of the Old Woman of Beare *33*

In The Staff-Room *35*

The Nestlings *38*

Pregnant *39*

Estate *40*

Evening after Rain *42*

Starlings *43*

The Solution *44*

December Love *44*

Miranda *46*

Love after the Fall *46*

Game's End *47*

The Bonfire *48*

from Absences and Celebrations (1982)

The Strangeness 55

Earthworms 56

Returning after Absence 56

Underwater 57

Not to be Born 61

Student's Window, Bath University 62

Chiltern Country 62

The Wave 63

Father 64

Newborn 65

Mother 66

Sleep 66

Odd 67

Taxonomical Note 68

Absences 68

Cool Medium 69

Reading Icelandic Sagas 70

The Disused Well 70

In Memory of Edward Thomas, 1878-1917 71

Appeals 72

Farewell to the Classics 73

Water Music 74

from Flints (1986)

Flints 77

Winter Wood 77

At the Open-air Market 78

Harvest 79

The Computer Room, Midnight *80*

Lessons *81*

The Hillside *82*

Small Incident in Library *83*

Blackbird at Dusk, February *84*

Frogs *84*

May Day *85*

Yobs *86*

The Visit *87*

On a Book of Nature Photography *88*

Three for Runners *89*

Postcard from Pembrokeshire *90*

The House Martins *91*

Meetings *91*

Say *92*

Blooding *93*

Squirrel *94*

A Local History *95*

Birds at Pagham *96*

Gaia's Dream *97*

Valediction *98*

The Haunted Road *98*

Not Daffodils *99*

Another Small Incident *101*

Marathon Man *102*

Outskirts *102*

Stellar Sequence *103*

Dune Country *104*

Something Else *104*

The Beechwoods, Autumn *105*

October Fungi *106*

Anniversary *107*

Lost *108*

Audit *108*

Finders Keepers *109*

from Settlements (1991)

Map-maker *113*

Scents *114*

Night *115*

For Beth *116*

Settlements *117*

Widow *118*

In The Playground *119*

Place-names *120*

On The Motorway *121*

The Anger of the Loving *122*

Relatively Speaking *123*

Vocabularies *124*

Haiku for a Lunar Eclipse *125*

The Maharajah's Well *126*

Paths *127*

Urban Grass *128*

Survivor *129*

Beth's Room *130*

Plural *131*

Against Geologies *131*

The Puzzle *132*

Hush-a-bye, Baby *133*

My People *134*

Prognosis *134*

Second Summer *135*

The Beech Tree *136*

At The Funeral *137*

The Dreamers *138*

From The Train *139*

Geomancies *140*

Barna-Oddr *141*

Naming The Moths *141*

Pen-friend *143*

Hedge *144*

Heatwave *145*

Doppelganger *146*

Envoi *146*

She *147*

Climbing to the Ridge *148*

from A Holding Action (2000)

The Lame Ant *151*

Once Upon A Time *152*

The Summer Country *153*

Accidentals *154*

The Cherry Tree *155*

Consider *156*

The Remembrance (May 8, 1995) *156*

January Night *158*

Amnio *159*

Daughter, Aged Five *160*

The Visitors *161*

No Answer *161*

Earth to Earth *162*

Success *164*

Lucre *165*

The Sleeper *166*

Endangered Species *167*

Limestone Pavement *167*

The Lost Weathers *168*

The Good Old Days *169*

Njal *170*

The Good Words *172*

The Birth of Poems *173*

Museum Piece *173*

The Birds *174*

Dolphin-watching *175*

Rejects *176*

Remembering The Picnic *177*

The Planet Happiness *177*

CV *178*

The Refusal *179*

Retirement *180*

One Country *181*

Novices *182*

from New and Selected Poems (2005)

The Programmer's Tale *185*

A Candle for Mr Sokolowski *186*

Embassy *187*

Heroic Ideal *188*

Beyond *189*

Journal *189*

Cosmologies *190*

Sixty *190*

Immigrants *191*

The Craftsmen *192*

The House *193*

The Woods *194*

To Air *195*

At Steep *196*

from No Through Road (2013)

No Through Road *201*

The Craft *202*

Acceptance *202*

First Night *203*

RTFP *204*

Blackthorn Day *204*

Parents *205*

Virtual Reality *206*

Rooms *207*

Expanding Universe *208*

Leap Second (31/12/2008) *208*

Slide Show *209*

January Morning *210*

Raggle Taggle *210*

Logos *211*

Language *212*

The Unforgiven *212*

Compromise *213*

So Soon *214*

Silva *215*

Riddle *216*

The Secret *216*

Red Kites At Shirburn *217*

On Learning Russian *218*

The Bards *219*

Another World *220*

Remembering Dido *221*

At Martlesham Church *221*

By Request *222*

Apologia *223*

At The Hospital *223*

The Last Walk *225*

from Unpublished Poems (2015-2018)

The Lost Land *229*

One afternoon of heat the express-train *230*

Constellations *230*

Afterlife *231*

67P/Churyumov–Gerasimenko *232*

History *232*

Encounter *233*

Centenary Poem for Robert *234*

Alzheimer's *235*

In Memoriam Roy Eagles *236*

Grandson *237*

Watford *237*

Homeland *239*

Stoic *240*

The Proportions of Pity *241*

On The Beach *241*

Moment *242*

Fragments *243*

Adonis Blue, Yoesden Bank *244*

So Long *244*

from Unpublished Translations (2015-2018)

This Spotless Child *249*

A Poor Girl's Funeral Cortège *250*

Clara d'Ellébeuse *252*

Departure *253*

Morphine *255*

My Day Was Happy *256*

Gudrun's Lament *257*

Autumn Day *258*

From her earliest years *259*

The Swan *261*

Song 8 *262*

Going Blind *263*

A Year Has Passed *265*

My Brother was a Pilot *266*

The Fox *268*

Index of Titles

from

OUT ON A LIMB

(1969)

OUT ON A LIMB

Someone had hung the rope there years before.
Tradition said Big Garry,
Who at ten wore long trousers and smoked,
And was later expelled from secondary school
For something no doubt terrible but nameless.
I would look up as a child at where it hung
Knotted to a beech bough, ninety feet above me,
A massive hawser, stolen perhaps from a barge,
Ending just short of the slope in a clump of knots
You could stand on, and so swing
Outwards from the hanger of the dell
Over a dizzying space, and back again.

How had he done it? How could anyone do it?
Terror would coil in my stomach just to think
Of his crawling up the near holdless trunk, along
That one flat bough, dragging the hawser with him,
Having to balance against it all the while.
And, as I stood, I felt my forearms tense
And tremble, till I forced them to relax,
Knowing that never in all my life
Could I do anything to equal that.

Still, if none of us could match the feat,
We had the rope to swing on. And we did,
All the long summer afternoons and evenings,
Spinning under the great green dome of the beech leaves,
Drunk with the rushing air, with the delight.
We vied in trying out new variations:
One would go round hanging by an arm,
Another upside down with legs entwined,

One by an ankle, – one even tried by his teeth.
(He unfortunately fell and broke his arm.)
Then there was this fir tree opposite.

The idea was to steer straight at it, then turn
By jackknifing the body at the last instant.
That could be tricky. Of course, the art of it was
To take the hawser back as far as possible
And get a good run down the slope for launching
So that the rope itself would carry you,
By its sheer impetus, as far as possible.
Even so, few ever made the loop
A perfect one, with neither buck nor sway.

Well, I can never remember growing tired of it,
But all the while there was this certain feeling:
However intricate our acrobatics
The flight that I was making was not my own.
Then there was this to think of, that the rope,
However strong it was, must perish some day.
Rain and frost were beginning to rot it now:
Sooner or later, it had to become unsafe.
Only one conclusion seemed possible,
Someone would have to tie another rope.

I couldn't get exactly the rope I wanted.
I didn't know exactly what it was,
Except it should be other than a hawser.
A different rope would have a different feel
Even if what it did was much the same.
So, I chose nylon. It didn't look so good,
But I wanted something durable and tough,
Light enough for me to carry up there,

And strong enough to swing upon, once up.
After a certain amount of private practice
I knew I couldn't put things off any longer
And went to the dell one morning, and stood for a while
Looking skyward up the smooth grey pillar.
It was slippery as glass and hard as iron.
Perhaps, here and there, one still might find a toehold.

I coiled the rope round my waist as best I could.
Barefoot, I began to climb ...

I can hear the wind. The trunk sways with the wind.
I sway within its slow gigantic circles.
All I can see is tree, and sky beyond,
A cold white light that moves and never moves.

I only look up. There is so far to go.

SEASIDE HONEYMOON

Walking today round the headland
We heard the hollow turbulence of the waves
Roaring under the rocks, and hand in hand
Descending egg-smooth boulders, found the caves.
When we came out the sunlight hurt my eyes
And now in the dark I see that dazzle still.
Bright shapes of a perpetual surprise
Meet and fulfil.

In the afternoon we watched the tide
Mount slowly to the rock-pools, saw the weed
Stir at the water's touch, while sea-birds cried
Flaking around us, coming in to feed.
Squadrons of light were moving out at sea,
Moving on the waves, intensely bright.
Night shall outride their silver cavalry,
But not this night.

Then in the evening we watched the island gig-race:
The sweat on the rowers' faces in the sun,
Puffs of air, patching the rippled surface
To smoothness, and the gigs gliding on.
They moved within a black and golden shadow,
In a timeless rhythm, thrust and follow through.
In the twilight the boats came home to harbour
And I to you.

Now in your body the tide is going out.
Over the shining flats the rivers run,
Leaving the golden thongweed to await,
Never denied, the sea's rejuvenation.
Now in the night my mind unfocussing
From brightness drifts to a great dark of sleep.
Still above the sea the white gulls wheeling
Cry to the deep.

WEDDING DRESS

You wore your wedding dress a single day,
Then put it off forever. That was right,
And it was nothing that you lost by night
That action symbolised. What passed away
And had to be relinquished was the hope
That all your life might now be virgin white.
While you kept such, one day that was not bright
Could set you longing for a vain escape.

You have accepted this. And now it lies
Folded away, in drawer and memory.
Yet you may find it, now and then, and see
With what was once unthinkable surprise
The buried garment, maybe hold it on –
That glad apparel of expectancy
Against the drab of your reality,
All your youth wore, unwearable again.

DIVISION

It is strange to think that to you I shall always be
Someone else, that however much we agree
In mind and body and however true
Our love may be, to you I am always you.

All men are islands, so it has been said.
But islands spring from the one ocean bed.
If the seas of our division rolled away,
What joined us might lie open to the day.

But then, what seamed and blasted wilderness
Might be uncovered, what contrariness,
What strange and stranded monsters. Better so
To keep the seas between us, not to know

What lies beneath what seems serenity,
Accepting that to you I am not me,
Content with what is visible above,
The green and fertile islands of our love.

TWO TREES

I saw where a crab-apple tree grew through a willow,
That was old and rotten, hanging above the river.
Its small lithe trunk matched perfectly a hollow
In the other's side; it clung there like a lover,
And all its branches were so twined around
And through the other's branches, one could say
Only by tracing both trunks to the ground
Which was the loveliness, which the decay.
And yet if the decay should die at last,
So should the loveliness be sure to follow
From having clung to it so long, so fast.
It was the crab that chose this way to grow,
It was the crab gave sweetness to the air.
The willow played its part, by standing there.

THE TREE OF FROST

Frost was on our world when we awoke,
Had furred the fences, floured coke,
And hung above the meadows like white smoke,
But cold, but cold.

Its bite when we went from the house was in the air,
A brittle silk cocooned dead leaf, and where
The world was winter-naked, frost had there
Clothed it with cold.

For as we went across the silver park
A chestnut-tree was there, leafless and stark,
But like a candelabra in the dark
Because the cold

Had turned it all to candles, made a wick
Out of each twig and stick
Coating it with this thick
White wax of cold.

And delicately now,
Vestal in the darkness, every bough
Was burning silently, as if some vow
Kept it from cold.

Almost I did not want to see the sun,
Knowing that by it this must be undone,
This crystal beauty turn to weeping, run
Relieved from cold.

But you, my winter-candled chestnut-tree,
Frozen so clear into my memory,

May you be ever such a light to me
In time of cold,

Teaching me that for all its winter days
The earth has not forgotten how to praise –
Teach me like you to stand so, so to blaze
Against the cold.

THE FLOWERS

Where others saw none, she would notice these,
The lost flowers of the speedwell in the grass,
White and blue, more delicate than porcelain,
The clear gay red of poor man's weather glass,
And on waste places mayweed after rain
Spreading its florets to the drying breeze.

Did they grow as things for her to notice,
Or was she there that she might notice them?
What did they mean, all those since childhood moments
When she stood gazing, as if root and stem
Had brought the flower to its shy existence
For her alone, as she was brought to this?

Too doubtful of the question for an answer
She was contented in her ignorance,
And afterwards, in her remembering,
The plants even attained a ghostly fragrance
Which was not theirs in any real spring.
And so in her they came at last to flower.

STROKE CASE

She sits in the sun, and smiles at the sun.
If smiling is that twitching of the mouth
And curling of the fingers. She cannot speak.
It could as well be weeping. People come.
'There, Polly dear, enjoying the sun?'
Or 'How are you today then, Polly?' Only
The tremor of her jaw betrays cognizance.
That much the stroke has left her. Still, the sun
Is hot today, and flickers through the beech-leaves,
And silvers the laurel, and the bees go humming
About the blossoms. Soaked now in the warmth
Of sun and wallflower she drowses, in a world
Remoter than the sun, perhaps seeing all,
Perhaps nothing, thinking perhaps of those two things
That are denied her, life and death, and now
Smiling a little, or weeping, at the sun.

NO OTHER ELEGY

All his village went to the funeral.
I never knew him well enough, it was
    No grief of mine.
But there was something in his way of death,
His being engaged, his lying in the road
    With a broken spine,
That I could not get out of my mind. At least,
It stayed there for an evening, while I pondered
    Vaguely on Fate,

Remembering how once at school, when I'd won a race,
He came in as I was showering, saying 'God,
    You went up that straight
Like a bloody bomb.' Now he'd gone like a bomb,
And bloodily enough, his life exploding,
    That motor-bike
Smashing him back against a telegraph pole
(No one quite knew how) in the night. But no,
    Old women may like
To draw a premonition out of innocence,
But I would just record his words as a kindness
    Spoken to one he hardly knew
Who was beneath him. And I'm afraid it's not much
Of an elegy for his broken life, but still
    What there is, is true.

THE RIPPLES

You troubled the still pool of my mind
Like a pebble dropped into it. And I was so
Intent on wondering whose was the hand
And what it was that made these ripples flow,
Outwards, questingly, as if to find
Something beyond themselves – how could I know

That into your mind too a stone had dropped?
It was the laws of motion in the end
That brought us into love. For as they touched
Our ripples hesitated, spread and widened,
Shivered to a singleness, then stopped.
Where now did the waters meet and blend?

SUMMER RAIN

Summer rain, falling all afternoon,
Turning the trees to green mist,
Soaking the railway cutting rhododendrons.
A frill of raindrops on their drenched mauve petals,
And the laurels water-polished.

And over the bridge go the blue-skirted schoolgirls,
With a twinkling of white ankle socks,
Their straw hats tilted to the summer rain.

LAMENT OF THE OLD WOMAN OF BEARE
after the Irish

I who was young am old.
Ebb-tide has come to me.
The days of my life flow outward,
The days of my life like the sea.

I am the Old Woman of Beare.
I used to wear a dress
Brand-new each morning. Now
I walk in nakedness.

When we were young we loved
Men; the girls today
Care for riches more.
The men have passed away.

Swift chariots and steeds
That bore off every prize –
Their day passed long ago.
Every good thing dies.

Look at these arms now.
They used to circle kings.
The bones stick through the flesh.
On them no wedding-rings.

The Stone of the Kings on Femen,
Mighty Ronan's chair –
Their cheeks of stone are withered.
How shall flesh ones fare?

Femen's plain I envy.
It has a yellow crop.
My crop is grey: I must
Wear this veil atop.

The waves of the sea are talking,
The wind blows up their spray.
Fermuid who was my darling
Will not come today.

I know where the kings' sons are.
They rowed across the sea.
Under the reeds of Alma
The lads that lay with me.

The flood-tide and the ebb,
The fluxes of the main,
I have known them all.
They will not come again.

The ebb is with me now.
No second flood will come.
I wait for the winds to be silent,
For the voice of the sea to be dumb.

IN THE STAFF-ROOM

' ... and Gillian Smith came in late. I was marking the register.
So I said to her, "Where've you been?". And she said, "It's my
        Mum.
She's bad again". I could see she was nearly crying,
So I said, "Would it help to tell me?" She just shook her head,
Biting her lip, you know, in that way children have,
And suddenly there she was against my shoulder,
Sobbing her heart out. I can tell you, it nearly broke mine.
I've never felt a child cry like it, and all the while
She wouldn't say a word, or couldn't. In the end
I did just manage to get her to give one smile,
And Janey West, who'd been hopping about all the time
Saying, "Please, Miss, shall I find her hymn number for her?",
Took her away. Tell me, what's wrong with her mother?'

'Multiple sclerosis,' said Rosemary.
'She's one of a family of five. The father looks after them.
The mother can't lift a finger. Literally.
She's in and out of hospital all the time.
We had a report on Gill. It said she was showing
"Separation symptoms", wetting the bed,
Doing this mirror writing – you know, backwards –
And wandering round at playtimes on her own.'

'Oh. I see.' She knew she didn't see.
After a while she broke out fiercely though.
'It's awful. But what is there you can do?'
'There isn't anything that you can do.
Oh, you can give the child affection. Not too much,
Or else it marks her out from the other children.
You can't be a mother to them all,
And so you mustn't try to be to one,
Even supposing that you really could.'

There was a silence while they drank their tea.
Outside over redbrick lavatories
Marbled rain-clouds dragged and drifted by.

'Of course, I'm still getting to know the class,
And yet I think I'd noticed her before
As having the kind of look that no child should have.
I do believe her face will haunt me now.'

Coming in, the headmaster overheard her.
'I don't know who you're talking about,' he said,
'But whoever it is, if you're going to take to heart
The troubles of every child you ever teach
You'll never live past thirty.'
                    'This one's different.'
'Oh, they're all different,' he said.
'Except there's never anything one can do.'
He sat across the corner of a table,
Looking out of the window over the playground,
Talking above the vague din.
                    'Take your class alone.
Eddie, as you've probably noticed, smells.
None of the other children want to get near him.
At the Christmas party they were playing Bigamy –

You know, this game where two girls choose one boy –
"Isn't this fun?" said Eddie. I heard him say it.
The others all got partners. He was left
Looking round, in the middle of the floor,
Wondering why no one came to him.
He's stupid, but he's not quite stupid enough.
He realised, and didn't understand.

So much for Eddie. Anne's from a broken home,
Lives with the father, a long distance lorry driver.
Came into school one morning very white.
Said that her arm was hurting. She'd broken it
The night before. The father was away.
She's only eight, she didn't know what to do,
Just lay there all night. Then there's Janey West.
Mother's a tart, all mascara and furs.
Hasn't much time for Janey, either way.
That kid's crying out for affection. Rosemary here,
She'll tell you how when she first had her in the class,
And took some notice of her, praised her reading,
The child hung round her all term, holding her hand,
Gazing up. It got so she had to be hard.
There's twenty-nine other children in the class.

Jimmy. You won't like Jimmy. Nobody does.
His father knocks him about. He pinches things.
He was brought to me once. He screamed like an animal,
Afraid I was going to hit him. And Peter Blair.
He came in once, showed me a photograph.
"Who's that, Peter?" "That's my Daddy," he said.
I knew his father. He left home when Peter was two.
"It's not now, is it, Peter?" "Well, it's my uncle."
"Why did you tell me it was your daddy then?"
"I thought perhaps my uncle was my daddy," he said.

Oh, I could go through half of them like that.
Annil Aktar. Annil's an immigrant.
Nice little chap when he came here. Great dark eyes.
The other kids call him Pakistani pest.
No need to ask where they get it. Of course, he reacts.
He can understand the tone if not the language.
He's turning vicious, sullen. Doesn't mix.
Let's face it. Half of these kids'll grow up delinquents.
What can we do? Is it our job to give them love?'

Outside the bell went for the end of break.
He slid off the table abruptly and dusted his hands.

THE NESTLINGS

This is the time of year one finds the nestlings
Fallen, lying on concrete path or lawn,
With the long pink legs trailed backwards, and the wings
Fledgeless, merest blotches of purple and fawn
On the flesh-pale sides. The heads are folded back
On the thin bent necks, the eyes
Open but never blinking at the black
Ballet of ants, the fumblings of the flies.

I have found them sometimes far from roof or tree
And wondered how they came there, whether thieved
By predator or left deliberately
By foodless parents. Being half-relieved
To find them dead, I try at least to fulfil
Some rite, as a child does, making each its hole
But troubling no more with crosses, and ignorant still
Of any fit prayer for the uncertain soul.

PREGNANT

Being pregnant was nothing so much as dull.
Far ahead loomed the Event, like a race she must run
On a course that she knew nothing of, and was unable
To imagine: a realisation like the sun,
Covered now with clouds of fear and uncertainty,
And likely when unveiled to prove too bright.
Being two people, she felt twice as lonely,
And on grey afternoons would have taken to flight
Anywhere, to be part of the world again,
Except that her burden would have gone with her.
In the fourth month her back ached, and the pain
Kept her from anything but watching the weather
And the passers-by. She longed for them to call,
Yet when they came she felt each word and glance
Directed at her body, that focus of all
Her life now, dragging everything off balance.
She, not this, existed out of sight.
And even her husband, when he came
Home in the evenings, tended her, and at night
Liked to feel it kick within the womb,
While she lay there stiff, as underneath a knife,
And understood now what this meant, to give
Or be given: that part of a life
Must die before anything can be brought to live.

ESTATE

Bulldozers draw the last stumps from the mud's slack mouth.
Some workmen in a group are mixing concrete
In a yellow mixer. I stand and watch grey sky
Come up above this edge-of-town estate,

Come up above scaffolded roofs and rain-pocked gardens,
The world revolving on a desolate axis
Of mud and broken bricks. What was conceived
Now quickens imperceptibly. From this

Yellow-pooled waste of clay, these tin tea-huts,
These piles of brick and lengths of mottled pipe,
Rags and linoleum and clumps of grass,
All that makes up this barren-seeming landscape,

The bricks shall slowly climb, themselves a stark,
Skeletal, unsentimental birth,
Waiting to be fleshed with all time brings
Between the sky's drift and the turning earth.

Think of that fruition, of that fleshing.
Think of the couples, mortgaging their lives
To debt and to each other, coming here.
Think of the wives,

Hanging out washing, talking over the fences,
Grown pregnant, leaning on the sink and staring
Past the back gardens to the woods,
Dreaming of spring.

Think of a thousand children, going to school
On a thousand mornings, enduring a million lessons,
Learning how to be bored, and how to enjoy
What boredom leaves. Think of the seasons,

Coming and going, bringing all kinds of weather,
But never so many days of sun or rain
As days like this, unmemorable, grey,
Yet with the rest not to return again.

And here will settle all the sediments
That peace permits: custom and occupation,
Those quicksands slowly swallowing our lives,
That nonetheless we take as their foundation.

And here will come the TV aerials,
Cars in the driveway, numbers on the gates,
Roses and chrysanthemums sharing front gardens
With stucco dwarf and dinghy – all that dates

An era afterwards, that gives its poignancy
Where nothing else – and what else will there be?
Beneath this shallowness, perhaps no deeper,
The acting out of a humanity.

For doors will be knocked, and what comes
Will never be quite what was expected or desired,
And some will die lonely in a darkened room,
Or live in one afraid.

And always there will be the sense of time,
The filling past, the lessening to be,
The sandgrains slipping through the narrow neck
Down into memory.

But here at least will be for some the place
That always they return to after absence,
The sacred ground on which are acted out
All the rituals of innocence.

And though to that sealed over earth no spring
Shall bring the blossoming of flower and tree
Still the blind sap shall not be denied
Its endless thrusting continuity,

As under this grey sky and in this time
The dumb assertion that will not despair
Begins again: trembling to be articulate
A rafter sways, then settles and is there.

EVENING AFTER RAIN

Nothing exactly says that it is evening,
The sun could be anywhere behind the cloud.
It is a matter of the daylight slowly altering,
The wet turquoise of grass and silverweed
Becoming slightly misty. Now the birds
Are tuning up; some single notes begin.
A bubble of rain is in the thrush's words
And will not loosen, till he ends his song.

And nothing indicates that if an evening
This differs from the evenings one has known.
Only some expectation keeps one waiting,
Counting in the twilight of the lane

The petals, as they close. Until the sun's
Disc drops suddenly: under the cloud
A whitegold sky, the elms drip light, light runs,
Rinses and dazzles, down the rainwet road.

STARLINGS

My father got up determinedly that Sunday.
'Those starlings had their boots on again last night.
I'll have to clear them out before they lay.'
I did not approve. But then I did not sleep in the room
On top of which they kept up such a brawling
And such a loving, in the dawn's small hours.

He poked a ladder up through the loft and climbed,
Descending some time later with a pailful
Of straw and mud, mixed with a few soft feathers.
('Breast feathers,' I said), the remnants of four nests,
And threw them in the hedge. And I suppose
He could not do much else; but later on
You should have heard the clamour as those starlings
Came crying desolate about the eaves,
Stirring us each with some uneasiness,
Their wings above the windows beating at
The closed doors of our pity or our guilt,
Like old wrongdoings, coming home to roost.

THE SOLUTION

The mind holds memory as a glass holds water,
And memory experience, like a sediment
That settles, in the end. This is forgetting,
This downward drift of all we found unsolvent
In consciousness: those grosser particles,
Though ready to be agitated, sink,
Followed by a fine silt of perceptions,
And what remains is – what? Not what we think,
Feel or perceive, but a capacity.
In the pure glass light's patterns weave and dance,
Trembling at their own serenity.
Always from experience to innocence
Time clarifies. Then is this the solution,
Our lives meant as a long distillation?

DECEMBER LOVE

The first time they went out was in December,
The twenty-second. As he walked her home
The pavements were alive with frosty glitter
And long clouds lay milk-white beneath the moon.
He was too shy with wonderment to think
Of anything to say to her, and she
Said nothing either; only their two hands
Maintained a gloveless contact in the cold.
Frost or this nearness made his whole frame tingle.
He wondered: should he ask her for a kiss,
But did no more than wonder, something held him

Spellbound and all of his desire seemed powerless
Against this sudden holiness of love.

Once on the way they passed some carol-singers,
Standing with lanterns underneath a porch,
And stopped to listen. '"Silent Night",' she said.
'I love that.' 'Yes.' Now they were nearly home,
And at the corner of the road where lamplight
Made sudden summer underneath the trees,
He stopped. She looked at him. He could not speak,
Only, taking her shoulders in his hands,
He kissed her awkwardly upon the cheek,
And then again, feeling her scented hair
Brush across his face, and through her coat
Her body trembling, whether for the cold
Or something else he could not tell. 'Tomorrow.'
'Yes,' she said, and that was all. They parted.
He walked home slowly underneath the stars,
And coming down the long hill from her home
Felt as if he could step off the earth
And walk instead the starlit avenue
That opened up between the drifting clouds.

Dreaming so, he came to the canal
And leaning on the parapet looked down,
Seeing the trembling stars suspended there.
The carol-singers could be heard far off
Proclaiming in the strange and holy night
The birth of love. He wondered what it meant.
Black as ebony and bright with stars,
The waters flowed beneath without a stir.
The church clock in the village struck the hour.

MIRANDA

For him, the storm-driven, her landscape
Was calm as cloud, seen at a summer distance.
He found a lightness there, that made him dance
In spite of grief. For her, it was escape
No less, into an infinite horizon
Of sky and sea, far from this island prison.

He grew acquainted with her winds and flowers,
Walking among her woodlands, in her valleys,
And she was soon accustomed to the sea's
Perpetual caress. In those first hours
He did not even know she was an island,
Close as they were, two wave-ribs on the sand.

Married, they sailed away. And she, Miranda,
Thought only sometimes of her seaward looking,
While he all but forgot his voyaging,
Who once was the sea and came with the sky on his shoulder
To her, the undiscovered still, the one
Whose green and endless hills stretched on and on.

LOVE AFTER THE FALL

Dwellers in a chalk and limestone country,
We never knew the well-watered valleys of Eden,
Whose Four Streams never ran dry,
The freshets and the fountains of that garden.

For long, it is said, we wandered in the desert
Where all the streams ran darkening into sand.
For survival, we sucked the damp grit
And in the dry storms held each other's hand.

Faithful we may have been, yet had no faith
To smite the living granite with a staff.
We were not the kind for miracles.
It was enough sometimes to hear you laugh.

And now we have come to our own territory,
No Eden, but the pastureland is good.
The waters flow here unpredictably,
But here at least is neither sand nor flood.

And we, the fallen lovers, knowing thirst,
Learned long ago to play the waiting part,
And have most joy in knowing after cloudburst
The winterbournes and swallets of the heart.

GAME'S END

On autumn evenings the children still play in the park,
Scuffing up the sweet-smelling aftermath,
Their shadows in the sunset triple length,
Making heroic kicks, half-legendary saves.
They play until it is dark,
And still for a little while after can be seen
By the flitting of their plimsolls, by their sleeves,

And by the twinkling orb of grass-stained polythene
Rising up white against dark sky or leaves.

Till by some common consent the game must close.
No one bothers any more to yell 'Pass' or 'Shoot',
Someone gives the ball a last terrific boot
Into the air and before it falls they are gone,
Wheeling away over the grass,
Snatching their sweaters up from the goalposts, going
Who knows where, only later to see how soon
The white ball never fell, but went on climbing
Into the dark air, and became the moon.

THE BONFIRE

And by the 4th, the bonfire was quite ready,
The central pole sunk in a four-foot pit
And wedged with flints; against its upper forks
Eight other saplings propped; these held secure
By interwoven crossboughs; finally,
Brushwood stuck in every interstice
And the hollow centre, that had been a camp
Where five could sit, or two hold against three
In clod and apple warfare, filled with boxes,
Paper, straw, a mattress and old boots.

On the next day only dew fell, damping
Nothing but the long grass in the fields
And after tea they all came out, the infants
Owl-eyed at the dark, the older children

Laughing and throwing bangers, but he the lictor
Bearing the torch of flaming tarry rag
Up through the smoky apple-smelling darkness,
Along the hedge, across the open field,
Under the wood's flint-dark and ferny leaf,
Till in the clearing where the bonfire was
They settled round him in a watching circle.

And he thrust the torch in low down through the side,
And in the woven darkness something stirred,
A glimmer, then a glow. He held it there
Till the whole structure grew alive with flame,
That licked along the interlacing twigs,
Became a sheet, hissed in the sappy evergreen,
Crackled up the dead leaves' fragile bronze,
And a gust of orange sparks whirled out and danced
Away beyond the trees. Then he stood back,
And the whole clearing sighed, and came to life.

There in the outer circle of the firelight
Dark figures moving in fantastic wreaths
Of green and ochreous smoke, fumbled with bottles,
Struck matches, hammered nails, or simply stood
In the leaping flamelight, wholly radiant,
Watching the dark-eyed, red-rimmed Catherine wheels
Slow to a halt from their brief spinning brightness,
The rockets, quaking out in coloured stars,
That wandering lit up the whole night landscape,
And the Roman candles, and the fiery spinners,
The flowering trees of silver sparks, or just
The flames themselves, reflected on the oak trunks
Or blanching on one side the clumps of grass
That on the other cast long shadow-cones.

But scorched and smoke-grimed, he saw none of this.
The fire possessed him wholly and was perfect,
Still retaining that tight outer structure
But all its inside burning in one blaze,
So that the boughs stood out like mullions
And transoms of a window, that one looked through
Into some realm where like a salamander
Truth moving in a furious bright ardour
Transfigured everything. He stood entranced,
Seeing an old boot blister in the heat,
Its tongue on fire and curling up; each eyelet
Glowing separately. And cypress burned,
Dropping wire-white flakes of ash, yet keeping
Its shape so long, a bush of fire, pure fire,
Till almost he would not have been surprised
To understand its hoarse and roaring tongue.

And to do that, he would have done anything,
Or anything just to have kept it going,
Short, that is, of throwing on himself
(Though even that darted across his mind)
Or others. Even so, he did his best,
Gathering leaves and twigs and clumps of grass,
Sprinkling them in a kind of benediction,
Knowing at least that it was little more.
And the flames sank low. He saw them idly
Reading the pages of an open book
He raked up from the outskirts, that before
They would have swallowed in a fiery instant.
Now they only blackened, line by line,
The type still standing for a moment, silver,
Then crumbling. And he saw a fallen crossbough,
On top still burning with a braid of fire,
But bearded with white ash beneath, and then

For the first time, felt the darkness near
Over his shoulder, looking at the flames.

And the last rocket stitched the dark with stars.
The fire sank to a bed of glowing coals,
That still the light wind drew sometimes to brightness
But could not keep from going out, and now
Only the centre pole was left still upright,
Like a tall totem, half-charred through,
But ready to come down at any moment.
Seeing this, he stooped and seizing up
A burnt log from the outskirts of the fire
Slung it low and sideways at the pole,
Which broke. Slowly it toppled, swinging out
Its bright arc, and it seemed the brighter then,
The motion turning spark to glow, and glow
Might have become flame, but it hit the ground,
Though in such starry ruin that the night
Skittered back wildly to the clearing's edge.
Then the flames died, and the shadows died.

Even then he might have stood, but rain
Finished the thing off, hissing in the ash,
And coming out of dream he found himself
Cold, the others gone, and knew that now
There was nothing left for him to do but join them,
Out in the dark fields, looking in the grass
For burnt out cases and spent rocket sticks.

from

ABSENCES AND CELEBRATIONS

(1982)

THE STRANGENESS

A strangeness is following us,
When it catches us we shall be gone
With steam and gaslight and the Inca cities,

An obscure generation,
Troubled, too numerous,
Bequeathing little.

Ah, but to be antique,
Our mint-new characters
Black-letter barbarous,

To live in photographs,
The crackle of old tapes,
And bundled letters,

And in our children's minds,
Barely remembering us
Before we passed from tallness.

Those, our inheritors,
What will they say of us?
How far our world, what strangeness.

How quickly, too, that distance
Will grow, till time's horizon
Cuts us off. Here then

A minor celebration
Made in time's despite
Of lost things, and the daylight

Of common afternoons,
Though none, beloved strangeness,
Remember or believe us.

EARTHWORMS

At the touch of rain they appear,
Welling from the raw ground,
Livid-snouted, paling to the colour of water.

I watch on paths and roads
Their slow self-pouring progress.
They die in myriads.

I spade my garden loam.
It crumbles clean and sweet
As old dark honeycomb.

RETURNING AFTER ABSENCE

Returning after absence
We were aware of strangeness
    In the half-dark room,
As if we had come early
Somehow, and chanced to see
    Time in its act of custom
Altering our lives.

These shapes we knew, that held us,
   Seemed as strange as starlight
Queered by far galaxies.
We stood there, scared by shadows
   Of a coming summer night.
I turned to look at you
And at the same time you turned too,
   Each thinking: was the other changed?
One unfamiliarity
Shaking our long close-joined reality:
   I saw you time-estranged
As time will have us, even that loved face
Grown indistinct within a shadowed place,
   Until we touched, and laughed, and knew once more
That we were haunted, but not haunters yet
With time ahead of us to pay time's debt,
   And you put on the lights, and shut the door.

UNDERWATER

On the pool's stone parapet a child
Counting to two hundred as he breathed

The water blue, opaque, swinging in panes.
Blocks of sunlight shattering against it.
The sparkles sliding and groping.
The small chest rising and falling.
Then rising, rising, rising.
Two hundred.

He got up and went to the water,
Swaying on the balls of his feet
Like a kite tugged by wind, like a balloon.
At the edge he sat down.

Warm roughness of glittery slabs
Under his thighs, on his hands.
Shouting and laughter all round,
A big coloured ball in the air
Spinning and everyone looking.
Nobody noticing.
Now!

He slid through the blue dancing panes
Like stepping through a mirror,
The bottom of the pool quicksilver,
White with the sun. Too much light.

Swim away down the slope,
Silkily descending
Like a spider, letting out thread.
This will do, here.

Water won't let you sit,
Pressure from beneath, tilting forward,
Go with the water, cradled.
Now all pressures equal.

Legs kicking by above
White like roots. No motion
Reaching here, only the rock
Of the water, only the clouds'
Shivering dapple, and noise
Far away like a fairground

In summer across a valley.
Settle down now, think.

What he thought of down here was up there.

He could see it all so clearly,
The girls with their towels round their knees,
The children running and shrieking,
The laughter of men like the beach-ball
Rising under the chestnuts,
Like the fountains, falling,

In the crystal ball of his breath.

He was neither warm nor cold.
The water crawled on his skin
Like static from rubbed amber.
Now, how long?

One minute twenty seconds.

Practising outside
He had held his breath three minutes,
Rolling on grass, tearing handfuls of grass.
None of that.

Air is turbulent:
Wind and the bubbles of blood.
Water deep down is calm
But the bubbles in the blood
One minute fifty seconds
Cry out still. The balance
Keeping the balance two minutes
Perfect at this moment

Shadow light and dapple
Lucid as possible
And the visions in the breath
A man at the moment of diving
O the arc of his fall like a rainbow
Flashing out over the water
Can't hold it can't hold it begins
Two minutes fifteen seconds
The terrible pressure to live.

Almost reluctantly
Beginning to drift up

Then sudden urgency.

How far. How far. How far.
He was bursting, sick inside,
He would never make it, fall back.

The sun like a white-hot magnet
Drawing him up through the water.
No more than a puppet now
Hooked on the wire of his need
Jerking, writhing, dangling.
Kick. Kick. Kick.

The last blue skin of water
Breaking over his shoulders
Surfacing to sunlight
The bright ignoring laughter
Everything as before.

Clutching the edge of the pool
Waiting for strength to get out

Pale-skinned convulsive frog
Limp, utterly drained.

Not amphibious yet.
Next time he would stay longer.

NOT TO BE BORN

No different, I said, from rat's or chicken's,
That ten-week protoplasmic blob. But you
Cried as if you knew all that was nonsense
And knew that I did, too.

Well, I had to say something. And there
Seemed so little anyone could say.
That life had been in women's wombs before
And gone away?

This was our life. And yet, when the dead
Are mourned a little, then become unreal,
How shall the never born be long remembered?
So this in time will heal

Though now I cannot comfort. As I go
The doctor reassures: 'Straightforward case.
You'll find, of course, it leaves her rather low.'
Something is gone from your face.

STUDENT'S WINDOW, BATH UNIVERSITY

Who, on some evening of spring, looks from this window
Or late at night curtains the loneliness
Of lit anonymous towns on dark horizons?
An answer: painted on one window-pane
In the round hand of almost childishness
'Anne's Window'. So it's you, my absent Anne,
Whose small room, high and barren, like a cell,
I use this night or two, and whose young head
My own replaces on this narrow bed.

I do not know you, Anne; we shall not meet,
And yet I ache with this frail almost knowing
That makes me see you over there, alone,
Caught in some moment far from common ground,
Poised in a soft uncertainty of growing,
Childhood behind, ahead the not yet found.
I see the tongue-tip, see the secret smile
As you begin to leave upon the view
That small affirmative, something of you.

CHILTERN COUNTRY

I was born in Chiltern country,
And the way that certain fields curve up to woods
That wait at evening, floored with firelit copper,
Is with me till I die.

Going back, you are still there,
Green folded countryside of copse and farm,
Where I would ride, long childhood summer Sundays,
The lanes to Chipperfield and Latimer.

Smells of midden, elder,
Thin honey scent of bluebells, old damp woods,
The long escarpments, distance-lavendered,
All is as ever.

Country of footpaths, small rivers,
Chalkland of flint and fossil, birch and fern,
How have you managed it? What chance or care
Has kept you changeless?

Green island, time is flowing. Now all odd
Enclaves are doomed. How long now till I find
That land no more, and lost in the world's changing
Ways that I, and once the Roman, trod?

THE WAVE

She waved, but he was out of sight, and so
The motion she had started in the air
Travelled on and had no place to go
That would have ended with his being there.

A thing so impotent, the hand's mere sigh,
Might, she imagined, easily be spent:
Lost among trees, dissolved in neutral sky,
Remote from meaning, come to be unmeant.

She turned away and kept her tenderness,
Not knowing how, immeasurably far,
A little of that unfulfilled outgoingness
Was in the fluxes that disturbed a star.

FATHER

Your coughing hurts me more. On winter mornings
And coming up the road it is your sign.
I see at last that you are growing old.
This summer you retired. Whose life with mine
Was mingled for so long and never noticed
More than as the flavour of a coat
Smelling of tobacco, as a forehead
Frowning at the desk-top where you wrote
Figures in a black book, adding up
To everything, to nothing, to a wage –
I whose youth so took your love for granted,
What answer can I make now to your age?

Father, it is too late. I want for you
All the chances that were never yours,
Summer ... but what can come? Only the summer
That autumn brings, the days warm for five hours
After the mist clears, and before the sunset.
Father, then I want for you no less.
Here in the autumn garden where you sit
Unlearning slowly an old restlessness,
Red admirals still tremble on the stonecrop
And swallows come, as to a meeting place.

Read now, remember, watch your children's children,
And fall asleep with sunlight on your face.

NEWBORN

Welcome, my defeat,
Soft as a fall into snow,
My most gentle undoing.
Your hands reach up to me
With innocent gravity
Drawing me into love.
I must enter the circle of cooing
And nest with the dove.

The violent and the swift
Break on you, soft rock.
Love reefs you round.
Now I must leave the ocean
For this one lake devotion.
Ah, sweet man,
My son, my calm encircled ground,
Today I too began.

MOTHER

I saw you in the small room stooped above
The figure in the cot, to tuck or kiss,
Your face made soft by lamplight and new love,
And you complete now, in your mother's bliss,
    Calling him honey, and rose,

But tired, never now to be quite careless,
And learning what love asks, and how life goes,
Custodian of a consuming brightness,
The old moon's shadow, as the new moon grows.

SLEEP

I am a mountain lake
That all day long the city
Drinks from, till I empty.
Drained, I lie awake.

Morning never brings
Again the brimful shining
To childhood dawns belonging,
Yet from night's hidden springs

Come now, sweet trickle sleep,
Flow in my mind and cover
This earth that it may honour
The contracts day must keep.

Sleep is starlit water
That drowns the stones of sorrow
And slakes the dry tomorrow
That comes when cities stir.

ODD

Odd how we live our lives:
When there's no trouble we worry,
Waiting for the moment
Of thrust, riposte and parry.

Queer fighting animals,
All doing and no seeing –
Why is it only action
Unsheathes the blade of being?

No hope now I shall join
Those rocks round which time rages,
The contemplative saints,
The calm cross-legged sages.

Something likes too much
That violent release,
Or something is afraid
Of what may come with peace.

TAXONOMICAL NOTE

Not just the sizes named (like miniatures,
Littles, queens, King Kongs, dwarf alleys, alleys),
But patterns, lovingly. Like silvers, clears,
Coca-Colas, bottle-washers, genies,

Sparkle alleys, squids ('thick squirmy patterns,'
Says my six-year-old), propellers, maypole
Alleys ('sort of stripy'), spiderwebs
And snowflake alleys ('they're most beautiful').

I tell you, there's a poet in this country.
He is probably eight years old. His head is full
Of coloured glass and words. He is a maker,
Unread, untutored, immemorial.

ABSENCES

Sometimes, when I turn my neck, my head
Explodes: just some ungristled vertebra
Catching, but that inward detonation
Sandbags my brain and makes
A momentary loss of time, a blankness.

Opening my eyes, I am surprised
Each time by trees, roads, houses, human beings.
How curious, how precious. I cannot
Resent their going on: whatever pact
I keep, they have no covenant with me.

I do not, though, much like these absences,
Which in no way resemble sleep, but rather
Miniature rehearsals, for that longer
Disjointedness when I am not, and what
Amazes is not likely to be these.

COOL MEDIUM

In fifty-three the children up our road
Got television and disappeared indoors
After school, instead of coming out
To toast crusts over stick fires in the hedgerow
Or fill the first-starred, batwinged dusks of autumn
With clamour of wild games. I sulked around

The silent woods, refused their invitations,
And hated ever since those moon-grey flickers
From a dead planet. Now, at night, I still
Walk past curtained windows, knowing each
Conceals that strange communion. Is life
Something to be given up for that?

Amused, superior, adult faces smile:
The awkward child stalks in the woodland still,
Keeping the ward of long-abandoned places,
As if one day the others might come back,
Stubborn in an antique heresy,
With trees and winter stars for company.

READING ICELANDIC SAGAS

In harsh communities close-linked as mail rings
They lived poor lives that we would never envy.
Starvation and disease, the climate, toil –
No wonder nothing grew in that thin soil
But one rare flower, a kind of self-belief
That rooted in the swarthy rocks of grief
And throve upon the air's salt enmity.
They lived like animals, and died like kings.

In mild communities that shift like shingle
We live rich lives that they perhaps would envy,
Well-fed and swiftly tended, sheltered, leisured ...
What flowers here?
                  A hope then, to be measured
By kinder virtues, maybe. Who'd regret
Those bloody settlements of honour's debt?
Pride's grown too perilous for us. How we
Lived, and met our dying, time will tell.

THE DISUSED WELL

Across the courtyard at the well's surround
The gaze went first to smooth-laid ferny stone,
And then was drawn through telescopic darkness
To something dimmer than a clouded moon,
Where deep down, long unvisited but changeless,
The living water moved beneath the ground.

Then into that dark shivering below
The guide let fall a pebble. 'Listen now.'
We listened, and long seconds later caught
The music of a faint awakened echo.
Our eyes met then, still mirroring some thought
That stirred within us at that secret flow.

IN MEMORY OF EDWARD THOMAS, 1878-1917

Between your pages so much lost was found
It seems a grief, that so much found is lost
To us who came too late and never now
Can walk with you and listen, as once Frost
Those summer nights. We see you ringed around,
As in the Malvern dusk, with friendship's rainbow,
Who never dreamed that you would haunt us so.
Inheritors, we mourn your lucid image,
Lost in the dark indifference of our age.

And yet, those pages say, you were as much
Alone, we are always alone, it is always dark.
Your days were measured by the willow leaf
And by the restless unreturning brook.
Lonely, you feared the salt demanding touch
Of others' love; night brought for all relief
The aspen tree's unreasonable grief.
Only one thing you asked for in the end:
That language should blow through you like a wind.

Now, on an April evening, I read you again
And hear your voice survive its vanished past.
I think of how my heart, at first encounter,
Leapt to you like a needle, homing at last
On its north, yet in your lines the rules are plain:
Be wary. Walk alone. Watch, and endure.
One remedy for all regrets is sure ...
A winter grief that quickened long ago.
Tonight I listen and the spring winds blow.

APPEALS

Almost daily the world
Bleeds through my letter-box. On the mat each morning
I find fresh gouts: blind babies, orphans, spastics,
The deaf, the lonely old, ill-treated pets,
Blue whales, otters, donkeys ... Donkeys? Well,
Why not; in indiscriminate despair
I scribble out the breakfast cheques, each careful
Conscience-minimum. Now world, will you
Leave me alone today? Will someone else
Apply these scraps of dressing? But the blood
Seeps through, it stains my fingers, sometimes at night
Becomes a bright unlaunderable flood.
Can't someone tell them I've a life to lead?
Just so, they murmur, drawing off, and bleed.

FAREWELL TO THE CLASSICS

Young, I followed these,
The dark shafts leading down
To tunnels, galleries.

I saw by a fitful torch
Of comprehension, caves,
Column, vaulted arch,

And roads, rubbled with years,
That linked a tribe, the tongue's
Untrafficked thoroughfares.

Something in that land
I looked for: was it life?
In the dark I laid my hand

On a child's forgotten toy,
And caught down corridors
Echoes of vanished joy.

Farewell the great rock-hives:
Time licks the honey clean,
Unsyllables all lives

At last. Homesick, I want
The towns of my own tongue,
These vocables still vibrant

With possibility,
These paths where I may meet you
That nothing roofs but sky.

WATER MUSIC

Here at the corner of the rock where sun
Silvers the wet rocks as the ripple leaves them,
In among the rocks and all around them
Soft bells of water sound a constant canon
Even in the calmest summer air –
The music of not going anywhere
That quiet water makes against the land.

Today we have come far among the rocks
Looking for coloured stones and bits of shell,
Hearing the lift and sigh of the long swell
Diminuendo down a thousand cracks.
Green water and a glow of amber stone,
The sun still burning, not much past the noon,
And music rippling all around my hand.

from

FLINTS

(1986)

FLINTS

We walk on whiteness, inches under grass.
Few would call it rock: these infant hills
Brittle as the bones of cuttlefish,
Will never last, they'll flow away like milk
In the next great rain and stain the tide,
And something will be left.
                      We dug a soak-pit,
Chambering the chalk, a well of white
Four foot deep and every bite the spade
Took of that smooth cake the tooth would jar
On something we must pry out: one more stuck
Flour-covered fruit-stone. There they lie, loose-piled,
Just as they'll lie a million years from now
Rubbling some scoured valley. Now my hands
That fought them loose fit lovingly around,
I feel for heft and socket-hollow, thumb
A sleek black shining.
                    Look, a tribe of dour
Dark-skinned aboriginals. They wait
Through bland white epochs, thick-skulled, underground.

WINTER WOOD

Coldest night this year, I walk the wood
At midnight in the warmth of singing blood,
Having drawn the curtains of my window
And seen the moon on violet-tinted snow.

No one else is out in all this land

Where silver birches doubly silvered stand
And oaks grown rowan-delicate unfurl
A winter blossoming of lace and pearl.

Puddles wheeze and blanch beneath my tread
But do not break; the branches overhead
Let crystal dust drift downward as I go
Through bracken fleece and brambles tyred with snow.

Stars burn greenly in the slate-black air.
Fox and badger do not leave their lair.
Cold is this kingdom, marvellous its light.
Nothing else will cross my track tonight.

AT THE OPEN-AIR MARKET

The long-haired huckster fans a stack of plates:
One pouring shuffle, like a waterfall.
Smells of crushed grass, frying onions, crates.
A crowd like driftwood builds against his stall.

Housewives mostly, ready for a lark.
He gets them going with a tale or two
Then settles to it, looking for a mark.
Beneath the smile his eyes appraise: And you?

Relax, friend. I'm not here to cramp your style.
Purveyors, like consumers, have their rights.
On with the foxy patter: I may smile
But only at a memory that lights

My mind up suddenly, like sun through mist,
Of how you once stole linen from a hedge
In palmy days when young wives could be kissed
Before life set your pugging tooth on edge,

And at another time how plausibly
With what aplomb you preached as you bestowed
Pigs' bones and pardons round the company
In April on the Canterbury road.

HARVEST

The field that started where my garden ended
Grew wheat and spring was green, a ribboned rustle
That silvered to the wind. But it was summer
We waited for: to rise in some blue dawn
And find the harvest started; on the hill
The cutter's wake of windrows, blond and glinting
Till baled and stacked they stood again in gold.

Shy as mice, we children watched from hedges
Until the workers went, then out we came
To battle on the slope with stubble-bombs
Or lug the bales to build, like chambered barrows,
Roofed passages where in the ripe hot dark
We sat exchanging stories, intimate,
Remoter from the world than Timbuctoo.

Did seasons last so long in that brown land?
We thought those harvest days would never end

And when they did there was another morning.
Yet autumn came: the wild green clematis
Turned to snow and coal-dust on the hedges,
The jigsaw pattern of the sunbaked paths
Melted, and the paths led out of summer.

Once though, my father took me where the men
Were working in the great barn, stacking up.
I watched them in the sunshot, moted darkness
And thought it then so fine a thing; there was
No play I would not trade to be as these
With salt-stung hands, sharing the harvest honour,
Least of, but known among, that company.

THE COMPUTER ROOM, MIDNIGHT

The air's cave-chill. You need two coats in here.
No seasons, nothing varies. Day and night
Walls hum, the white-tiled ceiling casts its light
On racked arrays; all's shadowless and clear.
For here's a place of clarity. And I
Inhabit it; secure I move between
These ordered oracles: see at this screen
I pause with midnight-hollowed eyes to scry:
At once the legend answering appears
Lettered in green fire: initiate,
I understand these matters; I dictate,
The strange beasts purr, obey me. Fifteen years
Of mastering these beautiful unmeanings,
Neat as a titmouse building nests of logic,

Conditioned by reward to run rat-slick
Down these electric mazed meanderings.
Time to go home. I sign the exit page,
Wish the guard good-night. Outside the dark
Is wild: great clouds rise up, a ragged murk
Obliterates the moon's faint silver rage.
I walk the empty roadways, I surrender
To masterless complexities of wind.
Back inside, the snowflakes of my mind
Are melting on the black boots of the future.

LESSONS

Watching these minds, more eloquent than mine,
Moved by their varied, passionate intent,
I offer what I can: extend, define,
And give, where nothing else, encouragement,
Silencing the sullen mid-life envy,
My own remembered lack, that says 'Too easy.'

The things I longed for and thought beautiful
Surround them now, and should it not be so?
What parent would not feed his children full
Or having yes within his gift says no?
Who'd teach them to be hungry and alone,
An old dog gnawing at truth's marrow-bone?

THE HILLSIDE

A hillside, through the hedge, like holy ground
Gold in evening sun. We find a gap.
The grass is lit or shadowed like a map
With molehill mountains. So, what's this we've found?
Such turf, bush-dotted; flowers everywhere
Like something from the great lament by Clare –

Chalk downland, undisturbed. Too steep for plough?
Yellow with rock-rose, flecked with milkwort's blue,
A knuckled whiteness where the flint shows through,
Here's dyer's greenweed, candytuft, and now
Too much – what's this that opens veiny leaves?
I kneel to it as one who half-believes

His luck at last, then notice by my knee
The level rays of sunset flash on brass:
An empty cartridge, glinting in the grass,
And feathers further on, and now I see
What keeps this place apart: some squire and friends
Down for the pheasant-blasting at weekends.

What's that, you call. Just people, at their games.
No, love, this is not paradise we've found,
But then, where's that on earth's old killing-ground?
My children course the slope, recording names.
I kick the cartridge, whistle them to see
Here where a green-winged orchid holds its plea.

SMALL INCIDENT IN LIBRARY

The little girl is lost among the books.
Two years old maybe, in bobble cap,
White lacy tights, red coat. She stands and looks.
'Can't see you, Mummy.' Mummy, next row up,
Intent on reading answers absently:
'I'm here, love.' Child calls out again: 'Can't see.'

A large man, his intentions of the best,
Stoops: 'Where's Mummy, then?' Child backs away.
Now the tall shelves threaten like a forest.
She toddles fast between them, starts to cry,
Takes the next aisle down and as her mother
Rounds one end disappears behind the other.

I catch the woman's tired-eyed prettiness.
We smile, shake heads. The child comes back in sight,
Hurtles to her laughing, hugs her knees:
'Found you!' in such ringing pure delight
It fills the room, there's no one left who's reading.
The mother looks down, blinking. 'Great soft thing.'

BLACKBIRD AT DUSK, FEBRUARY

Before the lambs and blossom
In the year's first lightening
   A dusk may come,

Not spring yet (frost on grass
Unmelted from the morning)
   But with promise

And something more: one note
Of hope beyond fulfilment
   Where a flute

Plays what all spring's sweet
Green accompaniment
   Cannot repeat.

FROGS

Blob on the lawn.
Black elastic flicker.
Blob on the path and the frogs are back, moving to spawn
In the spring night, travelling
By roads they remember.

Crouched in the dark,
Watching each quick soft rise,
I see in a garden long gone a child stooped to mark
Something unknown, not moving:
A yellow stone with eyes.

Strangeness, delight.
The lost world summons, near,
Softly electric, returning in leaps from the night,
My root-kin, my renewing,
At the spring of the year.

MAY DAY

Walking on the upland, caught by storm,
My son and I this May Day start to race,
Arriving at the same time, wet and warm,
Where valley beeches make a sheltered place.

Gossiping, our backs against a tree,
We listen to the downpour, watch the lane
Lilied with the swirl, dog's mercury
Drip and glister greenly, till the rain

On a sudden stops: grey-silver sky
Smokes northward, driven out by blue; we take
Our way again and move unhurriedly
Uphill just as the sunlight comes to make

A ribbed translucence high above and brings
Earth's odours steaming round us as we go.
Somewhere in the hedge a blackcap sings.
The wet bronze of the maple starts to glow.

YOBS

Me in the rain, my scooter broken down,
Fed up, pushing it, and these four lads
Block the pathway, jeering. Now, why's that?
No idea: for sure they don't know me.
I know them though (villages have eyes):
Petty vandals, go round daubing walls,
Snap the aerials off cars at night,
Wreck the children's playground, damage trees,
Tear the flowers up. Oh, I know them,
Know who's been expelled, in court. I know
Other things: I know who's unemployed,
Who come from broken homes, whose mother went,
Dumped him, four years old, to live with Gran,
I know who loiter now, unreachable,
By wasteland in the rainy winter dusk,
Who cry out 'Look at us!'
                              Not my affair.
I stand then, blocked, aggression's logan-stone
Poised, exquisite.
                        So, who's leader? You,
Tall, in leather jacket, skull-adorned.
'Afternoon. You any good with these?
My baffle-pipe's gunged up, I've sheared the screw.'
Silence. Jacket boy considers me.
Thinking what? We've got a right one here?
Puzzled? Wary? I don't know. And then
'Hey, look, what you do ... ' 'He needs ... ' 'No, look ... '
Hands in concert, octopoidal, blurring,
Strip, clean out, refit. I clear my throat,
Fumble in my pocket, find two pounds.
'Look, I'd like ... ' The leader, kneeling still,

Wipes his oily fingers, straightening,
Hesitates, then smiles and shakes his head.
The scooter starts first time. I ride away.

THE VISIT

Ahead, the others talked
   When the bus had set us down.
Four foot tall I walked
   The unfamiliar town,

And voices in my head
   Were speaking, grave and clever:
If the known should die, they said,
   The world will change forever.

That day of blaze and shade
   The tarry crooked street
Where once my father played
   Stood empty in the heat.

The terraced house was narrow,
   The stairs were dark and steep
Where children long ago
   Went candlelit to sleep.

Stifled in their cases
   The books inhaled again.
The photographs' dry faces
   Drank up my youth like rain.

And round and round the table
   Above the covert ears
The voices like a fable
   Were sighing for the years.

They might have saved their sighing.
   For all their child's endeavour
The known has died, is dying.
   The world is changed forever.

ON A BOOK OF NATURE PHOTOGRAPHY

This craft of light, as innocent as Eden!
The earth-star opening, the waterfall
Smoking from the basalt, blue-lit snow,
The wind-borne dust of catkins, green and gold,
A sun-caught fuzz of poppies – how they build,
These pages, to a celebrated world.
Here things speak for themselves within the frame
Of love's attentive silence. What's your text?
No theory you preach but practice, practice.
Beside the images laconic notes
Record a focussed being: angle, stance,
Precisions of the lens, the time of light.

THREE FOR RUNNERS

1.
A lace has come undone.
You kneel by the path in snow,
Aware of windless silence,
The body's pulse and glow.
Black cows by the fence
Stand and steam in sun
That brightens like a halo.
What words has joy? You run.

2.
Alone on the beach at sunset,
The blaze of sun on your face,
You come through curtains of light
To the lovely remembered place
And move like the mirrored gull,
Weightless, on shining flats.
The atoms of your body
Dance like summer gnats.

3.
Moonlight, rain, the road
A silk of shining gray.
Now all you ever were
And all that you will be
Fall equally away.
You are the road, dim-shadowed,
The leaves of that wet tree
Glinting and astir.

POSTCARD FROM PEMBROKESHIRE

My friends, who go so lightly here and there,
Who jet-propelled, car-catapulted view
Lands, cities, histories and never care
That none of it is yours or speaks to you,
I know you'd laugh to see me here perplexed
Still after two weeks by the rocks and seas
Of one domestic unfamiliar text
Missing my rooted etymologies
Of Chiltern beech. Yet there's no other way
For us, the slow ones, who would understand
The language of the summer clouds that lay
Their shivering allusions on the land.
We grow like lichen outwards, take an hour
To gloss the gannet's sky-and-ocean glide
Or lost in lexicons of tree and flower
Will walk daylong, while by the waterside
The dancing runes of river-light on slate
All but reveal the lost ... And summer ends
Before one sentence of it's learnt. Too late,
And yet today, out round the green bird islands
Where seagulls dipped to meet their soaring shadows
On sunlit cliff, it seemed to me I heard
Some phrase, one morning fragment ... Well, who knows?
I send my love, I'll keep that summer word.

THE HOUSE MARTINS

The night we quarrelled I went down to the beach
And twenty martins were there, weaving their flight
Under the sandstone cliffs in the last of the light.
Each had its own niche-moulded nest and each
Would leave in turn to twinkle, skim and dive
Then come like bees re-entering a hive
To hang in folded stillness. It became
Like a compulsion, counting each one back
To fit them in mosaic, white and black
Against the glowing cliff, or like that game
One plays with balls, for as the last flew in
So all the rest would tumble out and spin
In wider circles on the twilit sea.
Nothing I could do would stop that flight
Or lodge the last one in its nest till night
Called the birds back and brought them silently
To rest once more beneath the old scarred rock
That wind and wave had made a butcher's block.

MEETINGS

Sometimes behind the words of those you meet
You come upon a lost unshareable
Hinterland: some slate-roofed town, mediaeval
In morning light, a dalehead where they walked
Between moss-felted walls ... it's there so plain
You step like deer into this new terrain
Until you feel them falter, having talked

Some moments to you gone, so you return
From that deep journey back to surfaces
Yet ever after taste their lives like loss.
How can you tell them this? Unless, in turn,
You meet sometimes another watching too
Behind the words unshareable lost you.

SAY

Say that you're at work, and that it's summer.
July. The swifts cry out above the street.
Blinds are drawn against the light-dazed city.
    The office dreams in heat.

Say that there's a quiet dark-haired woman,
(Days like this, a man might fall in love),
With her wide quick smile to walk with you and sit
    At lunch with leaves above.

Say you talk together, oh, of nothing –
Dogs, yoghurt, husbands, children, wives,
Just the way we do that confidential
    Casual trade of lives.

Say you know, for all a million reasons,
Nothing is between you, nor could be,
That she is young, not even to remember
    The hour, your company.

Say you know it, but this day of summer
Touches you as soft as summer rain.

Light, leaves, her green and hazel eyes
   Work in you deep like pain.

Say, returning home, you sit that evening
At twilight under blossom on the grass,
Talking with your wife about your children
   The way such evenings pass.

Say that clarity returns, with laughter
For foolish love, but under it despair.
Say you know it now, that pain of sunlight:
   Your youth gone, hard to bear.

BLOODING

Coming back in late September twilight
After a good day out, the children singing,
A full moon yellow in the east and sunset
Dulling in the west above the cornfields,
We came on something in the quiet road:
A hare, run over, left to die, back legs
Smashed quite flat: a stuck moth, fluttering,
And yet not dead, but panicking wild-eyed,
Arching in the dazzle, pushing up
On boxer's shoulders, falling, pushing up.
No one spoke. My children looked and waited
Me? What competence had I in death?
I started off to let the car roll forward,
All set to do it in the modern way,
A filthy casual obliteration,
And could not: took a spanner and knelt down

Saying words. The great eyes rolled, went quiet.
I lifted it, the body cold as dew
Before I even laid it in the bracken.
No more singing. At the door my wife
Met us: 'What on earth ... ' My little one:
'Daddy couldn't help it,' ran upstairs.

SQUIRREL

Squirrel, like a blob of mercury,
Spills intact through cataracts of tree.

Squirrel's all but bird to nest and fly,
Walks on thin black twigs like cracks in sky.

Squirrel is half tail, a wave of smoke,
A plume, a catkin; squirrel's lord of oak

And walks the copse, not caring if he's seen.
Be prudent, squirrel, keep the trunk between,

But if you must forget, then be as now:
A woodland gargoyle, watching from the bough

As if to ask, 'What does it want of me,
That strange, untrustable, two-legged tree?'

A LOCAL HISTORY

Digging in his garden, someone found
A Celtic head, green-skinned, with faint smooth hair,
The nose fine-chiselled still, and beautiful
    The falcon stare.

North's the Roman road, but long before
The Ridgeway crossed these hills, oldest of lanes.
Blue cloaks, mud-spattered, gold-torqued warriors.
    The mud remains.

At Englefield the warboats of the Vikings
Startled the herons from their reedy bed.
Alfred attacked, drew back; the cold green river
    Received the dead.

Stephen and Matilda: Wallingford.
The winter land cried out for God's relief.
In the beechwoood's grey cathedral trees
    Put forth new leaf.

King Charles's men, by secret furzy ways
Came south by here to fighting in the town.
Richard Atkyns mourned his men 'like fruit
    The wind blows down'.

Records for last century: one winter
Five babies dead, winds cold, much frost again.
Water from the ponds, mud floors, the roads
    Milky with rain.

Beside the recreation ground a cross:
There died so many, from so small a place.
Still among the old a few remember
   A name, a face.

Nineteen eighty. New estates, new people,
The easeful lives of rootless liberty,
While the stone head watches, and the woods
   Wait silently.

BIRDS AT PAGHAM

Sunlight on our backs,
   Redshank, dunlin, plover
Braid with looping tracks
   Mud the tide will cover
Brimming to embrine
This level liquid shine.

Out above its flow
   Two herons in their flight
Billow as they slow
   Long-legged to alight.
An avocet, sedate,
Crazed-china-delicate,

Trawls the pond. All's birds:
   The south wind from the sea
Speaks with curlew words
   Of limitless and free

Bright unpeopled plains
Where solitude remains.

Shivered waters glint
    And now from reeds close by
Five arrowheads of flint
    Go spanged across the sky:
Snipe turning in the height
To vanish into light.

GAIA'S DREAM

Even now, there are places that remember.
Here, where the rocks are rounded to the north
And sleek as seals from that old polishing,
Where valleys end mid-air, sawn-off, and lakes
Sudden in the hollows under crags,
Flash like kingfishers, the earth will dream.
They come back then. A million blue-white snails
Rasping their way with boulder-studded tongues ...
Their licks and furrowings disturb her: see,
She shivers in her sleep, the sun has gone,
The wind is from the peak, the lake's still eye
All pupil now stares inwards, black, opaque.
Ten thousand years are buried in that blink.
And where are we? Diminished, back to scale,
A scattered few, precarious in caves,
Enduring at the edges of her dream.
Again she cradles us with cruel love:
Her latest kind, whom she might come to favour
Or else, tomorrow, might scour off for good.

VALEDICTION

My children grown too old for lap to nestle,
Affection now must play the manly part,
Concealing in the clasp of hands or wrestle
The touch that has been rain to this dry heart,

And I, like all progenitors, discover
Time's paradox: how permanent each stage
Of childhood seems to parents, until over;
Looked back upon, how fleeting all that age.

Now words must take the place of love's first language
Of touch direct and simple as the sun,
And I in colder orbits find the courage
That love must look for, when its work is done.

THE HAUNTED ROAD

That was the route I loved best
In all my running: a road
Hollow between high banks
Where the farm carts took their load.
The moons of after-harvest
Shone on the dust and showed
Embossed each glinting grain.
The haystack's reek in winter
Was summer's breath again.

That road was haunted, they said:
A tall dark man would glide
Out of the shadows and move
Keeping pace at your side.
A hood would be over his head,
If you spoke he never replied
Till looking down you would see
Whatever walked beside you
Ended at the knee.

No ghosts kept this boy back,
Not then, though the hairs of the young
Rose in the pitch-dark hollows
That the hedges overhung.
So now, shall I fear the track
Or those I walk among,
Though keeping pace they glide:
My escort of the shadows,
The dark man at my side?

NOT DAFFODILS

Less pleasant now, to lie,
Half-dreaming, half-awake,
And watch with inward eye
The images that break.

Not daffodils, my love,
But falcons of remorse
Attend me from above
And track my desert course,

Or water rises fast,
A dark and closing sea,
Where present joins to past
In salt complexity,

Or else that fire, once out,
New-kindled in my brain,
A winter wind of doubt
Extinguishes again.

Air, water, fire: which leaves
Another element.
That image also grieves
And is not heaven-sent.

My love, I hear you claim
It's what you've always said:
That small good ever came
From idling on a bed.

Come then, and exorcise
My vacant, pensive mood
With your clear outward eyes.
People my solitude.

ANOTHER SMALL INCIDENT

November evening, rain outside and dark
Beyond the building's honeycomb of warmth.
The old man stands there, waiting to be noticed.
He wears propitiation like a coat.
The girl looks up at him. 'Yes? Can I help?'
'This card you sent like, that's the problem, see.
It says I've got your book, but that's not right.
I mean, I had it but I brought it back.
That's what I do, I read one, bring it back.
I never keep them, see.'
                              He stands, condemned
Yet quivering for justice. 'All right, sir.'
She smiles at him. 'We get mistakes like that.
Just leave the card with me.' He stares at her,
Seventy, with spotted hands, afraid,
And someone smiles at him and calls him sir.
Lighting at the contact, like a bulb,
He warms to her. 'That's what I do, you see.
I take the one, I read it, bring it back.
I thought, you know, it might be on the shelves.
I mean, if no one's had it since like, see?'
Another girl comes by. 'We're closing, Sue.
You coming?' Sue looks up and rolls her eyes.
The old man catches it. He understands.
He turns and shuffles out into the night.

MARATHON MAN

On stone-hard spirits, lichen.
How do they fare when it starts,
When the legs fail and the heart's
Great labour flags? What then?

But you, John, stayed the same
For dying you ran still
Though slowed by death's long hill,
On which last road you came

To a place known to few
Beyond all hope and pride
And did on that far side
Such things as you could do.

OUTSKIRTS

Someone should speak of these peculiar margins,
Neither town nor country, where nobody goes.
The cornfields seem abandoned, yet corn grows.
The pasture's shaggy, like a firing-range.
Who cares for this, who keeps it? One begins
To wonder sometimes. I have stood at twilight
Watching swifts around an empty grange,
Black boomerangs, returning in their flight
So close their wings have clipped me. There's a fear
About this. Where has everybody gone?
Almost comforting the ridged horizon

Contains the motorway's lit pouring sea.
Even so, I do not go too near.
It would not do to risk a certain sight,
No traffic there but wind, and endlessly
The shining pistils stretching into night.

STELLAR SEQUENCE

Young stars begin to burn as though
   There were no limit to their light
And they alone were charged to show
   An old defiance to the night.

In middle years the helium
   Contracts, but now in novel ways
From dark disequilibrium
   Some breed a self-consuming blaze.

These shells of radiance depart.
   They sink upon themselves again.
A pulse reveals the signal heart
   That chafes in its compacted pain,

As now with all their lustre spent
   They turn to night a secret face
Yet grow in their diminishment
   Till time is bent about their place.

DUNE COUNTRY

    Crouched, I become the land
Flexing its lion shoulders. The light torments me.
Something's far out, it dazzles on the sea.
    The wind comes, driving sand
Minute by minute, bearing my substance away.
How shall I root and stay?

    I stand my shifting ground.
I build defences, knit with marram, heal with moss.
The sift, the scurry, whisperings of loss
    Continue all around.
These brambles with their blood-dark leaves, their fruits are
mine.
They taste of mud and brine.

    Gulls glitter in the height.
Men, when they come, are the odd ones, walking alone.
The sea brings driftwood, delicate as bone.
    I drum to gales of light.
Wind tears my roots, throws down my building, all's in vain.
I lie low, try again.

SOMETHING ELSE

Once a day, at lunch time, for an hour
I leave the small hot cabin where I work
To walk this land between the road and river
Unclaimed, or little used: where fields of grass

That nothing grazes flank a muddy footpath
Beside which runs a culvert filled with brambles,
Tyres and stagnant water.
                            I have found
Nothing here remarkable, unless
One counts last winter's snowdrifts on the bank,
Lipped and fluted, like great smooth-gilled fungi,
Or else the flocks of gulls that came to feed
Beside the shining thaw, and always rooks'
Black flaking storms, or pigeons' floating silver
Between the poplars.
                            Nothing then, and yet
Something has happened: like a child returning
Affection never known the land has answered
My love's wry constancy: the blackbird now
Sips at the puddle while I pass, the bank vole
Patters from the ditch, and I have found
In spring marsh marigolds beneath the bridge,
Gold on dark green, in that place a thing
Amazing: giver and receiver both,
The land and I, stand back in gratitude.
We know survival; this is something else.

THE BEECHWOODS, AUTUMN

Stillness, like a trance of time. We look
Down avenues of silver, listening.
There come these days, more beautiful than spring,
Calm as a reflection. Nothing's far.
Perspectives flatten: look, love, here we are

Safe in an illuminated book,
Gold leaf and shafted light, with one green spray
Patterned on the blue ground of the sky,
Or see us quaint as in a tapestry
Walking under trees' brocaded silence.
So autumn has renewed our innocence.
How can this end? No word is said: a ray
Travels back and forth, a rainbow dancer
Between two trunks on threads of gossamer.

OCTOBER FUNGI

They are back again, the people of the woods,
A travelling circus of freaks: they have pitched their camp
On meadows of moss between the boles of beeches.
There's no concealment here: they loll on stumps
In sulphur tribes or swagger in the leaves
Scarlet as outlaws. Fear is in their names:
Destroying Angel, Deathcap, Sickener.
The darkness bred them, devilry's their lore
And parody their style. There's Dryad's Saddle
Perched, a monstrous butterfly of leather;
This velvet sleek translucence is Jew's Ear,
There's blewit's ghostly lilac, polypores
Rubber-tough or textured like meringue,
Smelling of peach and honey. So we meet
Towards another year's end in the woods.
What shall I say to you, gay-sinister
Consorts of corruption? Welcome, life.
The slugs have gorged themselves on stinkhorn jelly

And here's a puffball ready to explode,
A wrinkled cerebellum, parchment-yellow,
A rotted sack of flour that splits and spills.
The spores rise up, dream-delicate, like smoke.
They glint and dwindle down the shining air.

ANNIVERSARY

A rapids-rider, finding this brief stay,
No more perhaps than where the waters gather
In amber calm before the next cascade,
I turn and see, surprised at my surprise,
(Unthinkable it could be otherwise)
That you're here too: have threaded your own way,
So close yet separate, by shoot and boulder
Through the daze and din of time's white water.

You smile again with that old innocence.
I think: the springs of youth did not foretell
These cataracts ... I dreamed you swan-like, made
To drift beneath green courtesies of willow,
Your cygnet brood unendingly in tow.
What brought you then to such a turbulence,
Time or I? Yet we are here; the swell
Draws our craft together. All is well.

LOST

A joke among the family: how father
Gets them lost, then cheerful in disgrace
Speaks for the virtue of the unplanned venture,
The vagrant interlude, the unsought place.

Who found the fallow deer, the brambly clearing
Where berries hung their tartan tapestry?
Who came out on the cliffs that April morning
Above the hammered silver of the sea?

Ah, but had they come where they going
What then would they have seen, their counter goes,
While he pursues the path of his unknowing
To 'Where's this?' answering 'God only knows.'

AUDIT

Being middle-aged is closing doors.
You owe too much: consider the expense.
The sign the people look for is not yours.
These rooms that you keep ready – where's the sense
With guests so seldom? Come, abate your pride,
Confess it now: this is not justified.

Then pull the covers over, draw the blind,
Look round for one last time, and turn the key.
They never came, the ones who might have dined,
So was it loss, that hospitality?

Disdain such reckoning, though doubt and age
Are frowning at the items on the page.

FINDERS KEEPERS

All was to be revealed,
    Labelled and exact,
As on some site lies peeled
    Each layered artefact,

But memory, you prove
    No archaeologist
So patiently to move
    No crumb of life is missed.

The flashing random spade
    Ungovernably delves.
Who thought to see displayed
    Such debris of lost selves?

Stranger, should there glint
    Upon this ruined scene
Among the clay and flint
    Amazingly washed clean

Some relic, then receive
    If lost indeed be found,
The right of trove I leave
    To this my troubled ground.

from

SETTLEMENTS

(1991)

MAP-MAKER

There ought to be a survey done, with maps.
One shouldn't come upon them unawares.
I mean the places where you fall through time.
You know them by a lifting of the hairs,
A sudden tense alertness, not quite fear,
The air's electric whisper: *who goes here?*

It happens anywhere: an old canal,
The corner of a field, a cobbled mews.
I'd plot them all, a pointillist of time.
I've worked it out, the colours that I'd use:
Vermilion for the present, shading back.
The past's autumnal spectra end in black.

My maps would be a handbook for the haunted.
There'd be blood-red, then, for the motorways
With cities in their web like scarlet spiders,
But over here, in delicate flint-greys,
High on the downs pure Neolithic time
In chalky hollows, lingering like rime.

For furthest back, before the glaciers,
I'd let sloe-purple paint the night of caves.
My Roman ghosts would rise in blues and ochres
And Bronze Age russet glint about old graves.
How lovingly I'd chart one valley's scene
In Saxon gold and fresh mediaeval green.

But there's no school for time's cartographers
And any skill of mine to mark and keep
I'd lavish on the contours of the living.

It's only sometimes, at the edge of sleep,
I watch imagined colours pulse and fade.
How beautiful, the maps I never made.

SCENTS

Tonight the rain in summer dark
Releases scents of leaf and bark:
The fumy reek of resined trees
And currant's sweet acridities.

Those aromatic compounds fit
Some membranous receptive pit
And trigger in my waiting brain
The memory of other rain.

I learnt my seasons from no class:
My summers were wild rose and grass,
A velveted and honeyed air.
Tonight I know: the past is there

And lies, so little does it need
To live again, in bush and weed
A yard or two beyond my door.
I am the child I was before.

Odours of earth, like love they came
Before the word, before the name.
The gates of time swing wide for these
Primaeval analeptic keys.

Then let me keep, though all depart,
These strange familiars from my start:
As in my first, in my last air,
Most potent molecules, be there.

NIGHT

Night is another country, like the past.
   I study there,
Learning how small a light will do at last:
   A muffled moon, one star,
How puddles in the blackest winter night
   Will spread a blacker glimmer, how the frost
Will lantern leaf and twig with haloed light
   To guide the lost.

I've watched, a darker shadow from the shade,
   Five badgers pass
Like broken moonlight moving in the glade;
   I've come on deer at grass
And fled with them the blind assaults of cars
   Like flash-floods in the gully of the lane
And waited till the only light was stars
   And seen again.

The unlit land is in me: when the towns
   Are loud with day
I close my eyes: a night-wind from the downs
   Has cleared the mist away.
The god I make myself is deep and still,

Absorbing all, an endless starry dark.
I hear the train far off behind the hill,
   The farm dogs bark.

FOR BETH

Dearest arrival, what a time to come.
Just when the party was over, never a doubt,
For children change, my love, they must go out
From the haven of our help, tall sons become
Voyagers: that's it, never again,
I thought, that trust, that sweet enquiring talk.
Families grow, like petals on a stalk.
Time is a wind that plucks. A gentle pain:
The years, I called it, nothing to regret.
We never thought, or dared, to ask for more,
Yet now you come, a small one, to our shore,
Time's compensation, our last gift and debt.
Sleep then, my daughter, on this guarded strand.
None ever came more welcome to my land.

SETTLEMENTS

In those days you were always moving on
To the place that didn't need you, to the town
With its milling squares and grey aloof cathedral
Or the village where the memories went down
So deep the conversations of the old
Were roots of willow threading time's black mould.

And the places took no note of you, or smiled
Seeing you come, intent on reverence,
But then retired, to business or stillness,
Behind the stone facade, the pinewood fence.
Where can the young belong? What can they own?
You travelled onward, unaddressed, alone.

Yet sometimes you would stop beside the road
In a place that was no place at all, you'd say –
One shuttered shop, a forecourt hazed with petrol,
The heat and silence of a summer day –
And voices would be round you, conjuring
The gift of something you alone could bring.

Or on the upland maybe, in a field
Where history had never been at all
You'd stop to shelter from a burst of rain,
Crouched in the nettled angle of a wall,
And feel about you, like a beating heart,
The dispossessed, unwilling to depart.

And you would stop your ears, and turn away:
Was this the heritage for which you came,
The edge of things, the spare, the unobserved,
All that had lost, or never knew, its name?

Somewhere another kingdom lay in wait.
You hurried on towards your true estate.

You are older now. You have your own domain,
A narrow land, but country of your choice.
It blurs a little, known so long, so well,
But not the other. Clearer now the voice
Of all that sought you, heavier the debt
You cannot pay, or own to, or forget.

WIDOW

Twelve years alone. I watch time hunt you down.
Each meeting now, another earth is stopped:
Some building gone you knew from long ago,
Another friend to visit, lying propped
On death-ward pillows. What I do, I know –
The Sunday calls, the lunches in the town –
Weighs in the balance lighter than a leaf
Against the steady boulder of your grief.

I listen to the worries of the old:
The forms they send you, buses that don't run,
The closing shops, the tradesmen that won't call –
The genteel expectations one by one
Fall from your life. I listen to it all.
I counsel: have your comforts, don't get cold,
As if what tracked you were not sure and slow
And colder than a winterfull of snow.

Another place, another century
There might have been a solace for your kind:
The corner by the fire, the gathered children,
A life, to be recounted and refined.
They would have honoured you, that otherwhen:
Curator of the tribe, great mother-tree,
The rooted one with ripeness on her bough.
Your tribe is scattered: who will honour now?

We part. Again you tell me not to come
If roads are bad, if I've too much to do.
I reassure. I drive off in the dawn.
'You've got your job to get to.' Yes, that's true.
The pulpy silence of the winter lawn
Will start to beat within you like a drum.
I've left you something: cups to clear away.
You'll read the paper, wash up, face the day.

IN THE PLAYGROUND

A small one bumped his knee.
Another came to see,
A girl, with no defence
But clumsy innocence
Against another's pain.
She tried and tried again
To make his crying stop
By pirouette and hop:
'Look what I can do.
Now I've hurt myself too!'

The small one stopped and laughed
And she too, at her craft;
But then became aware
Of someone watching there
And blushed, as if for shame
That he should see her game
Who might not understand.
She took the small one's hand
And they were gone, unknown
Like fish beneath a stone.

.

PLACE-NAMES

'The place-names all hazed over
With flowering grasses ... '
      Philip Larkin, 'MCMXIV'

They are worn and durable
      As silvered oak,
The old names: Coombe and Barton,
      Stow and Stoke,

Burying the land
      Leaf-litter deep,
Gorgeous as Arundel
      Or plain as Steep.

Improbable on signs
      The past remains:
A Norman lorded here,
      There died the Danes.

That dyke the Saxons dug,
   This river-name
Murmured its light sound
   When Caesar came.

Bless the namers, men
   Of pen or plough.
History, receive
   Another now.

Poet, labourer,
   They do not pass.
We scent them on the map
   Like new-mown grass.

ON THE MOTORWAY

Lonely on the motorway, the light
Fading fast and eighty miles to go,
I conjure ghosts to travel with tonight
And see you there, your cigarette aglow,
No different for fourteen years of death,
And neither of us wholly at our ease,
As if we went to speak, but held our breath,
The way it always was. At last, to please,
'Nice car' you say. I shrug, indifferent.
You know we've judged life otherwise again,
But now for once I see your good intent
And what it overlies, the hidden pain.
We never talked. I know you wanted to.

I drew my silent pentacle around.
It would have hurt too much to let love through.
Too late, I'd ask you in now to my ground.
'I never understood ... ' A silent touch.
The darkness turns. 'Was it like this for you:
That all you did seemed never to be much,
But what you did was all that you could do?'
You nod. 'I'm sorry.' 'Don't be. Children learn.
You think love's ever wasted?' Something bright.
The cigarette is gone, next time I turn.
I travel on, alone again, through night.

THE ANGER OF THE LOVING

The loving should not anger.
   They know the price of rage:
The mind upon a tether,
   The heart within a cage.

And if it were tomorrow
   The end of love's delight,
That time should bring a sorrow
   To stretch the minutes tight?

The loving should not anger
   Nor lie apart in pride
Like hills across a water
   Though side by touching side.

All pride and domination
   Are folly of the weak,
And still we let time tauten
   And only silence speak.

RELATIVELY SPEAKING

If we could have time slower
   Our longing might arrest
And keep the lightning's flower
   Dendritic, silver, pressed
On night's black slate forever,
   But love is dispossessed.

If we could have time faster,
   Our knowledge by such speed
Might have the coming chapter
   And all time's book to read
Till starlight's tale is over,
   But time will pay no heed.

Since no art yet can alter
   That enigmatic rate,
Upon a steady river
   We travel, yet await,
And understand time's answer
   Too soon, or else too late.

VOCABULARIES

Like stars, or swarming bees, or flocks of birds,
We think them hardly countable, our words.

Yet fifty thousand's all we use, it seems,
For truth and lies, reality and dreams.

Which puzzles me. The world's more things than that.
Do languages grow lean as lives grow fat?

Is so much absent from our brains and eyes?
What's lost, I say, when we economise?

There's too much difference we make the same.
All poets love the miracle of name

Yet mourn exactitudes they cannot state:
The single noun that might denominate

Their moods of quietness like falling snow,
Or yearn for lexicons they cannot know:

The speech of eagles, what the dolphins sing,
The glossolalia of leaves in spring ...

Nothing, we dream, could bring us to content
But fifty million words for what we meant,

To fit whatever happened like a glove,
Redeeming lost pluralities of love,

Until we wake to truth, and see again
Unharvested, like leagues of sunset grain,

Outnumbering all stars and bees and birds,
The matchless universe beyond our words.

HAIKU FOR A LUNAR ECLIPSE (17/8/89)

On the shining rim
What crimes do you foreshadow,
Fingerprint of Earth?

Look, an ice-cap grows:
The glaciers of darkness
Burying bright lands.

Inexorable arc –
Yet when were these night's colours?
Rose, viridian.

Come, dark ferryman:
Lightly on the shining eye
Earth lays its obol.

Where the lily was
A bronze rose has unfolded
In night's old garden.

Stillness above all:
The stars for lack of moonlight
Burn more steadily.

THE MAHARAJAH'S WELL

I love this well, that stands among the trees,
Gorgeous-preposterous, like a bower-bird,
With its cupola of chocolate and gold
Topped by a burnished spike, like the twist of a turban,
With its shining elephants, and scroll of carp.

It was Ishree, Maharajah of Benares,
That wrote to Edward Reade, Lieutenant Governor,
Born in the Ipsden country, friend to Benares
Through years of famine and mutiny, missing always
A far-off hamlet lost among the beechwoods,

'Edward, that story you told me troubles me.
To think of a child being beaten for stealing water!'
(The melt of glaciers carved out our valleys;
Since then no stream's endured: the waters glug
And vanish through the fine white sieve of chalk).

'Ours is a dry land too. Let a well be sunk
For our friendship's sake, and the sake of your people at home.'
And so it was done, in eighteen sixty three
By Wilder of Crowmarsh, a foot for each day of the year
Hand-dug through chalk and perilous shored-up gravel,

And the Maharajah paid, and Edward Reade
Bought land, appointed a keeper, raised an orchard,
And bonfires blazed in the Maharajah's honour
That none need trudge again, raw-handed with buckets,
To clay-lined ponds half-choked with weed and rush.

Now this is true: you can go and see for yourself,
Since virtue is always surprising, like an oasis,

For the Maharajah is dust on the thirsty plain
And Edward Reade came home and departed at last
Into the dry-leaved silence of the beechwoods,

And water was brought by pipe: the well was barred,
But the dome is there, by the road among the trees,
And the shaft remains: if they let a bucket down,
They could draw up water still from the aquifer,
It would tremble again in the light, it would quicken and quench.

PATHS

What country has such paths? Our maps are green,
Reticulated like an insect's wing.
I love those veins. I trace them, summoning
Salt-road, flint-road, holloway: each scene
Rises responsive to my finger's course
As dot and dash pulse out their living morse.

These are the roads that talk. No tarmac here
To gag time's voice. That rut, that blue-rubbed stone,
Those polished roots say footsteps not my own
From immemorial kept my paths clear.
I see that long procession, race on race,
Moving before me at time's proper pace.

I'd follow it: look for me, if you will,
On some brown pathway like a spit of sand
That lakes of bluebell lap on either hand
Or on the green road where it mounts the hill,

The drover's road: I'd like to fall asleep
In wind and sunlight, counting vanished sheep.

But mostly under beeches look for me
Or listen where my rustling feet would cross
The paths that moonlight knows beneath the moss.
My shadow will be sharp ... How can this be
Denied to me: was I not all my days
A woodlander and keeper of the ways?

URBAN GRASS

Last of the green companions, grass,
You stand at bay in nature's pass
With banners threadbare but unfurled
Against a steel and concrete world.

In strip and square, on dusty banks,
In trodden, flayed, polluted ranks,
On arid marl and burning clay
Your long resistance wears away.

What Sparta bred you, not to yield
One acre of the stricken field,
Though none lament, where you obeyed,
The stubborn, democratic blade?

Or does the wind bring news again
And is it told about the plain
In some ancestral singing home
Of fog and fescue, bent and brome?

I dreamed earth had its honour too
That lived, for all that we could do.
I walked saluting in the street
The armies that will not retreat.

SURVIVOR

What's lost each century? The one before.
He's ninety. Quieter, he says. More green.
I glimpse it through him like a closing door.

He calls with things: a book, a magazine.
Can't stop, he says. Sits down, deplores the news,
Drinks coffee, talks of countries that he's seen.

Pressed trousers, overcoat, black shiny shoes.
He brings the children gifts: a joke, a sweet.
They listen to him but the clothes amuse.

How could they comprehend the long retreat:
But in good order, like a Guards' brigade,
Acknowledging withdrawal, not defeat,

Though all the roads run seaward? He has stayed
Too long he says, won't do; shakes hands; steps out
Stiffly; late, you'd think, for some parade.

BETH'S ROOM

The new room's finished. Standing at the door,
I show my infant daughter where she'll sleep:
No curtains yet, or carpet on the floor;
A smell of paint like apples; sun; a deep
Unpenetrated silence. Yours, I say,
Forever, or as long as children stay.

But what's a room, demands her wide-eyed stare.
Why, love, a piece of Outside we make In,
A complex annexation of the air,
The property of stars, till we begin
To fence a little space with wood and stone
From all the universe to be our own.

Or say that it's a vessel, like an ark,
We load with life, that loud menagerie,
That bears us through alternate light and dark,
Our place of trust, our island on the sea.
Here you will sit: your longing and your love
Will fly from this wide window, like a dove.

And so it waits, this threshold you must cross,
Your second (for the first was into life),
And other rooms await you, to my loss,
But far off yet are womanhood and wife.
How still you lie, to watch the sunlight fall
And our two shadows, mingled, on the wall.

PLURAL

It's birth begins it, our disunity:
From one to not-one, so we learn to count.
Fingered by the first mists of infinity
Two is a signpost where the numbers mount
Up past all eyried crags by Cantor's track
To what no mind can visit and come back.

Who was it though? What prophet, mage or king
Was first, the very first, to dare that land?
What thunders pealed, that day of reckoning
We took the integers from God's own hand,
That starry knowledge, heavier than stone,
And came down-mountain, plural and alone.

AGAINST GEOLOGIES

Our seconds rain like shells of lime
To build great thicknesses of time:
We watch the secret moments fall
Anonymous beyond recall,
Since who will look for you and me
In those white beds of history?

But if they do, with prying pen
When all our now has turned to then,
Let them not think, because they find
Some particle we left behind,

They know the vanished sea above
That was our salt and sunlit love.

These words I leave for them to learn
Like lily's stem or print of fern
Are but our shadow in the stone
And all the rest is ours alone.
Then what a world of touch and talk
Shall lie compacted into chalk.

THE PUZZLE

Granted that we have it, this recall,
That at some random needling of the brain,
A word, a scent, roses will bloom again,
The dead walk in the country of the skull,
The puzzle still remains, so often, why
Our minds select the things they do for these
Synaptic resurrections: why those trees,
That patch of grass, a gate, some drizzling sky,
The time and place forgotten? It's as though
Something within us shies from too much sense
And counters it with pure inconsequence,
And yet they seem like things that we should know:
From days, perhaps, when all we did was live
Rapt, irrelevant, unpurposive.

HUSH-A-BYE, BABY

All right, dear, I'll not risk bad dreams again
For our small daughter, singing her to sleep
With my sad ballads. Now Sir Patrick Spens
Can stay dry-shod; Queen Jane shall not cry out
For Good King Henry in her agony;
The channering worm shall chide no more; fair Janet
Must leave her truelove to the elf-queen's keeping,
And Arlen's wife will absolutely not
Be pinned right through the heart against the wall.
Henceforth, as you request, I shall confine myself,
Like any normal dad, to nursery rhymes:
Strange egg-shaped characters will smash themselves
Irreparably; ill-housed, harassed mothers
Whip hungry children; babies fall from trees;
Mice shall be maimed; sheep lost; arachnophobes
Fare badly; innocent domestics suffer
Sudden nasectomies, and at the end
We shall dance rosy-faced in a ring and drop dead
        with the plague.

In either case, outside the small lit bedroom
The glass shall weep with rain, the winds be howling
Their old, uncensorable savageries.
But you are right, of course: we should choose well
What songs we sing, to lull them for a while.

MY PEOPLE

My people never tell their love:
   Love ends where revelations start.
They keep it tethered like a yacht
   On private waters of the heart.
Some evening on the twilit roads
   They slip their moorings and depart.

That narrow craft each mans alone
   And none that watch those sails unfold
May know what skies are borne away
   Slow-gathered in the silent hold,
Nor if, upon another shore,
   Love makes a landfall, and is told.

PROGNOSIS

The matchless reflex of the eye
   Must lose its speed, the wrist its skill,
And that attacking swordsman Time
   Move like a dancer for the kill.

How measured, how mesmeric-soft
   The footfalls of his sure advance.
No stop withstands, no counterthrust
   Can fault the logic of his stance,

And others, better men than you,
   The brave, the quick of mind and feet,

Fell back before him to the wall
   That leaves no possible retreat.

No declaration then, no deed
   Shall move the master of the bout,
Yet some, I hear, have troubled him
   With what might almost be a doubt,

As if, one instant at the end,
   The pure resistance that they made
Perplexed the cool ironic eye
   That studied them above the blade.

SECOND SUMMER

That was the summer when you named the world.
I'd push you round the lanes or carry you,
Your small face eager, wanting to be told,
And me too anxious, sometimes, for your due:
I wanted so much for you, mountains, seas,
As if it weren't enough for anyone
What I could give: one village with its trees,
Its cooing doves, its verges hot with sun,
And all around it, fold on secret fold,
My watchful land, the silences of moss,
The meditations of an ancient loss.

What did I think imagination needs?
Were Edens never nondescript before
With tarry fence and yellow wayside weeds,

Or had I grown too tall for love's first door?
Ah, when I thought I took you by the hand
Who was it led the other one to see
By lane and bank the lost enchanted land
Forever in its wordless mystery,
And when you blew the clock of silver seeds
That says that time is always and the same
Which of us taught, which of us learned, the name?

THE BEECH TREE

Ten years ago I lay in hospital,
Not ready for it, tense, unsociable,
Stopped, as I had not been since I was born.
There was a tree: I'd wake to it each dawn,
All seethe and glimmer by my window pane,
And through the hot days turn and turn again
To where that house stood open: there were rooms,
Stairs, translucent attics, raftered glooms;
I'd lie beneath the lifting silken eaves
And feel the sunlight on my skin of leaves
And when I slept, within me I kept furled
The web and lattice of a secret world.
Not easy for my kind, the stubborn odd,
To ask the ministry of man or god,
But this at intervals for these ten years
Has come back to my mind, sudden as tears,
As if I lay again, too taut to breathe,
Then heard beyond the glass the gentle seethe:
My green physician, waiting out the night
To labour at the alchemies of light.

AT THE FUNERAL

Funerals of the old are for the old:
The young, even the middle-aged, intrude,
Stiff in their unpractised piety,
Distracted by oak poppyheads, by light
From stained glass windows blue as irises.
There may be grief, but they are grateful too
To simplifying death that has unpicked
This knot of care from their much-tangled lives.
It is the old that mourn without alloy,
That shoulder loss and lay it to its rest.

Who are they though, so lusty at the back
With lifted voice, needing no book of hymns,
The sad spruce women and the grey-haired men?
What is it that they stare at past the air?
Outside, in winter sunlight, all's revealed:
The cousins of her youth, friends, neighbours, come
To honour old acquaintanceship; now lives
Like long-divided rivers meet again,
A swirling confluence of memory
Carries the dead one to the final sea.

How gently they exclude one. 'That would be
Before your time.' 'That's going back a bit.'
But always to such time they do go back:
To rationing, the Blitz, heroic toil,
The fields of childhood, legendary snows,
Shops, terraces long gone. I understand:
Each dying nerves a new resistance, firms
A final bond of shared exclusiveness.
This is a closing ranks: like pioneers
They man the dwindling circle of their days.

The January sunlight has turned cold.
The ceremony's over. They depart
Down unsafe streets to doors they must keep locked.
What they came to do is done: somewhere
A girl they knew is running over grass
In a green country, leaving them behind
To counters and containments, ritual
And stoic unsurprise, such as they use
Whose lives have fed on long adversity,
Who know betrayal, and will not betray.

THE DREAMERS

At night the strong field of the mind
That keeps our single world defined
Relaxes: then in dreams we see
Like fruits upon the quantum tree
The endless worlds of parallel,
And we are interchanged a spell
To live by that strange picture-show
The lives our waking cannot know.

For there in that infinity
All things that could have been must be.
So nightly we explore the ways
Of time's enchanted mirror-maze.
There on the paths we did not take
We meet the friends we did not make,
Embracing beautiful regret,
Or wake in danger's deadly sweat.

But this the cosmic censors keep
Fast locked behind the doors of sleep
And minds that tauten to the light
Forget their nightmare and delight,
Not knowing in what bliss or pain
To worlds of morning once again
They wake, those others on the tree
Who dreamed that they were you or me.

FROM THE TRAIN

From the train at dawn, on ploughland, frost
Blue-white in the shadow of a wood.
Oh, you again, of all moods soonest lost
And most elusive and least understood.
What should I call you? Vision? Empathy?
Elation's tunnel? Worm-hole of rejoicing?
Some bliss of childhood, reasonless and free,
The secret microcosms ... What a thing
To have no name for, yet to live for, these
Curious contentments under all,
These moments of a planet: weathers, trees –
What dreams, what intimations, fern-seed small,
Are buried in my days, that I must find,
And recognise, and lose, and leave behind?

GEOMANCIES

Like a careful Chinese geomancer
I play the game: *where shall I build my house?*
As if my days and money left more choice
Than standard boxes, twenty to the acre.

Good omens, said that craft, were cradled mound
Within the long blue curve of dragon hills;
A southern upland, where the sunlight falls;
Let water be before you, trees behind,

But keep yourself from pathways that are straight
And shun the level plain, the naked rock
That loose the secret arrows of ill luck ...
O gentle masters of an antique art,

What would you answer now, when all crafts falter?
Where shall we make our dwelling and our path,
Afraid of the deep poisons in the earth,
The sickness in the wind, the death of water?

Sorrow in all lands, and grievous omens.
Great anger in the dragon of the hills,
And silent now the earth's green oracles
That will not speak again of innocence.

BARNA-ODDR

He figures briefly in a near-forgotten
Viking saga, bearer of history's
Saddest nickname, Barna-Oddr.

Which means 'Babies' Odd, and was given him because
He objected to a game his companions had
Of tossing children up and catching them
On the points of spears.

No more is heard of him. It is not known
How often, if at all, his spoilsport will
Prevailed. Only one thing is certain:
There were never enough of his tall, dissentient kind.
But those there were should be remembered, who had
No words of caritas, no star, but only
Uncertain, dangerous imaginings
Stirring in their brutish minds, that things
Were better otherwise; who stood and spoke
Their flat, sword-hilted 'No.'

NAMING THE MOTHS

'You'd call me poet? Hardly, Sir,
   Arms and the man I did not sing,
But once upon an August night
   I named the Yellow Underwing.

'We found on language's great map
   A little corner, left all blank.

Such handiwork, without a name!
  (The Maiden's Blush has me to thank).

'How I recall that dew-damp eve
  Of honeysuckle-scented June
When first upon the Silver Y
  I set the summons of man's rune.

'I see them now, our haunts of old,
  Our hedgerow banks, our woodland glades,
Like memory itself they flit,
  My Early Thorns, my Angle Shades.

'And some, you say, would honour us?
  Then, Sir, I am obliged to you,
But such was never our intent.
  We did what seemed our own to do.'

Swifts and Ushers, fold your wings
  Softly on the moonlit land.
They who loved you best are gone,
  Walking somewhere, lamp in hand,

Seeking down eternal lanes
  Moths the angels might have missed,
Proffering before the Throne
  'Some Amendments to Your List.'

Willow Beauty, Burnished Brass,
  China Mark and all the Plumes
With the Footmen gather, dance
  Lightly now above these tombs.

PEN-FRIEND
for Yang Liuhong

A girl, a poet, writes to me from China
In quaint uncertain English: in Beijing
Is spring, the trees and grass begin to green
But wind and sand too much, the sky is yellow.
In Beijing autumn is best season: then
The sky is blue, the Fragrant Hill is red,
The Red Leaves red, the mountain is like fire.

Not sure how much she'll understand, I write
In quaint uncertain English back: I say
Here in my country also it is spring,
We have blue flowers underneath grey trees,
The stars last night were bright, I do not know
What stars shine on her country, I am sorry
I cannot write in her own language back.

She sends me poems someone has translated.
Her dreams are white: white coral, moonlight, snow.
Soon, she says, she understand me better,
Then she translate me: I become Chinese.
This grows too strange for my imagining:
Whom shall I meet now, on what fire-red mountain,
Talk with, in what yellow windy spring?

HEDGE

They felled the hedge today:
   Hawthorn, tree of twilight,
A green cliff, streaked each spring
   With waterfalls of white.

Now let the voles unlearn
   Their lanes of leaf and bough.
What musty dark will keep
   The hedgehog's secrets now?

And let the birds lament
   Their sanctuary and store,
The redwings that will come
   To the coral feasts no more.

What autumn now shall light
   Their flare-marked landing-strip?
Tonight the hurdling wind
   Forgets its rise and dip.

It is only the eye that stumbles
   At a step no longer there,
The ear, alert, that listens
   For the long surf of the air.

HEATWAVE

The world's less real on summer afternoons.
We walk in dazzle, wan as daylit ghosts.
The streets are white and foreign: in dim shops
Assistants idle, sheened like melting wax.
In offices, in schools, in hospitals
The hours are burning dunes, and far off yet
Oasis evening with its water-dreams,
Its shadows and its cool solidities.

The countryside's no better: mirages
Sizzle on the surfaces of lanes;
The larks vibrate in poplared distances;
Crops swelter in the fields, on crumbling banks
The soil lips back from blue-white teeth of flint.
All roads are longer: air lies honey-thick
Round farmyard gates; a solitary child
Puddles its naked foot in pavement tar.

Truth is, this is no season for us now:
Untalking and untouching, we endure
Like cattle on the hillside, till day's ebb
Sucks at the round-pooled shadows of the trees.
'For the young' we say, disturbed at light
So riotous and squandered, suited now
To cooler, more reflective husbandries:
Night, and the moonlight's pure economy.

DOPPELGANGER

Old doppelganger, image in the glass,
Appearing like a witness as I pass,
You startle me, return my rueful smile,
Then settle to a pool of pure attention.
How candid still you look, so free of guile
    Or comprehension.

And how reluctantly you testify,
Though made by law to meet my level eye.
Your gaze is – what? Propitiation? Shame?
As if you would embrace me, like a lover,
But cold between lies what I cannot name,
    Nor you discover.

ENVOI

Most grow out of it, but now for me
It looks as if it will not end till death.
Some stubborn spring is wound too tight inside me
That cramps my gut, denies my words my breath.

So, the foolish, daily fight goes on:
People avoided, kindnesses unspoken,
Little salvaged but the desperate pride
Of those who are always defeated but never broken.

Also a little knowledge: how the world
Treats us, the grotesque, the vulnerable:

Its laughter, or surprising charity.
It is for certain faces most of all

In street or shop, the gentle, the perceptive,
I make these words that I shall never say
To stand for how I hope I might have acted
Had others been as I, and I as they.

SHE

She inhabits our furthest silences.
   Her coming is like thunder
In gathering, electric distances
   Or the freckle of first rain.
Sometimes, walking in the winter street,
   You breathe her promise, like a sharpened air.
Listen, she says, be watchful: we shall meet.
   No hint of when or where.

So little time, of all the time that's ours,
   With her; so long to wonder
Where is she now, amid the stumbling years,
   And will she come again?
But then to meet, and all be as before,
   To read the question in her changeless eyes:
Do you ask more? No, Lady, nothing more
   And nothing otherwise.

CLIMBING TO THE RIDGE

A little while, to climb the ridge again:
The body flowing, smooth, on reels of silk;
Wicks of cotton-grass in winter sun
Luminous; red moss; the soil's black butter
Salted with white sand.
      A little while
To see through wind-gapped mist the fields below
Gleam like ocean shoals, the lake a spearhead
Barbed and tanged with light.
      A little while
To lie back under white sky; hooded, sleep;
Wake from warm throb to the kiss of snow
And come down-mountain, careless, like a rock-fall.
To say: where does it go?

Beyond the edge of hearing curlews cry.
The pools, wind-shivered, wait for others now.
What is there here to mourn?

Your song is in the silence.
Your stone is on the cairn.

from

A HOLDING ACTION

(2000)

THE LAME ANT

I have known those who were kindly, not because
They had anything to gain, or thought they had,
Not even, it seemed, from a consciousness of virtue
Or principle of faith; one might have said
Such was their way, from an overflow of gladness
Or because the innocent heart keeps open house
Scorning defence, but anyway, so it was.

I have thought of fairy stories: how they teach us,
Against all reason, that kindnesses return,
That when the king's son seeks the giant's daughter
What wins the quest is the irrelevant rescue
Of certain wayside ants, who later come
To do the task that he cannot, and gather
The seed the giant has scattered, each last grain.

And I have wondered what part I might play in this,
Knowing myself a grown man, middling hard,
Watchful of my defences, a dour accountant,
Weighing and balancing. And I have thought
That if nothing else I could be one of those
That gather and give back: the lame ant, maybe,
Who brings the last seed in before the nightfall.

ONCE UPON A TIME

The corn-ghost walks at twilight with yellow hair.
In the wood are watching faces, made of leaves.
Set cream for the boggart, silver for the elves.
Beware the black dog on the road, beware
The green-toothed hag of the pond, devourer of men –
So, in an old lost darkness once, we wove
Tales like the firelight, born of fearful love:
A shifting, shadowy propitiation
Of unknown things, the world's fierce otherness,
A lessening of mortal loneliness.

For man is lonely, but the credulous
Have company: fish sing to them from streams,
Birds counsel them, to them the Elf-Queen comes
In her skirt of grass-green silk; it is they who pass,
Bearing their fern-seed, into the fairy hill
For the one night that is seven years beyond.
The feather-cloak is given to the earthbound
And the magic beans are destined for the simple
Who trade their one possession, yet will see
The morning garden green with mystery.

But this was long ago: the world's great childhood
Is over now: those shadows love and fear
Are back within us, where they always were.
They served us well, the goblins of the wood,
The talking wolf, the witch's house of bone,
Taming our night with names, while flowers sprang
Where beauty walked, when the old tales were young.
Now they are done, and we are back alone
On the cold hill, with one true tale to weave
That we shall answer for, and must believe.

THE SUMMER COUNTRY

It is August: we are back in the summer country
Caught in a queer sunlit time-warp, watching again
From high cliff paths slow-circling buzzards weave
Their invisible basket of rushes; skimming flat stones
Across a cream-and-turquoise sea; caressing
Lichen's impasto rock-maps; talking late
On honeyed evenings under buddleias,
For this is what we do in the summer country.

We root again in lost simplicities:
Tonight down at the bay I watched the moon
Rise full and hang above the headland, blazing.
The tide was on the turn and wavelets spilled
In scallops of slow silver; when I ran
My shadow flew beside on moonlit sand
In shared immortal fleetness, as if none
Grew old or weary in the summer country.

It is the children belie us: last year's babies
Run up the beach with towels round their heads
Whoo-oo-oo being monsters; toddlers then
Scale rocks; the restless teenagers have gone
Like coracle adventurers. Then we,
Are we not changed? I think, now that I look,
Your auburn hair this year a little whiter.
Is it the sunlight of the summer country?

No, it is telling us: a time will come
When the calm clouds will build above the ridge,
The brassy heads of knapweed nod and shine
Beside the high paths where the buzzards wheel,

The footprints of a wandering breeze will print
A sea of peacock silk, the sun's reflection
Fill trembling pools with trellises of light,
But we shall come no more to the summer country.

The evenings darkening, a touch of frost,
Mist on the sea: love has such home-turnings.
Only, let it endure: let others come
As we have come, each year, to these innocent edges
Where the bruised heart is healed by apple-dreams.
More we do not ask: the bright sand settles,
Leaving clear water as the wave withdraws,
For so it happens, in the summer country.

ACCIDENTALS

Fourteen years ago this spring I saw
On a windy day when the white of cherry-blossom
Startled against grey cloud, at the edge of the wood
Where hornbeams grow, a flock of hawfinches
Bold, many-coloured: a gang of swaggering pirates
They dropped from the trees' high rigging with cutlass-bright
    bills
Strutting the leaf-strewn deck; I watched and they
Allowed it: are we ever so honoured as by
Such pure indifference?
                        I have been back
To the wood each spring, but they have never returned.
Life is short for most things: comets, rainbows,
A fall of moonlit snow; one can only be grateful

For the rare conjunctions, for the accidentals
And grace-notes of existence; can only listen
For the once heard, though never heard again.

THE CHERRY TREE

The cherry tree was doomed, but trees die hard.
It lay beside the woodland path, blown flat
Three months before, the evening of the gale
That threw our beeches down like pick-a-sticks.
That April it still blossomed: you could walk
The whole length of its trunk from airy roots
Through bridal, overarching boughs to find
What only birds by rights had found before:
The secret cave, a waterfall of stars.

The bark of burnished leather peeled like satin.
Look, I said, it's over now, the headsman's
Waited his time, but still she kept composing
Her petalled elegy, that woodland queen,
Putting on, for robe of execution,
The finest of her green gowns, trimmed with lace.

CONSIDER

Consider how they move, the galaxies,
Through the ocean of night like driftnets
Dragging deep space, though nothing we know is there
To be caught in that radiant star-knotted mesh.

Consider how they pass through one another
Like ghost armadas: let the stars be ships
A million miles apart: still that belittles
The loneliness of those bright galleons.

Consider light: by that same token see
A snail track silverthreading black Saharas
Between the stars, yet nothing anywhere
Outpaces that immortal messenger.

And then consider: who shall know us, what
Companion us: in all the shadowed room
What hands might cup this candle, flickering
In time's wind, in the vast forever dark.

THE REMEMBRANCE (MAY 8, 1995)

We crowd the hilltop, standing in loose ranks,
A thousand, maybe, come from all around.

Scents of hawthorn, woodsmoke, trampled grass.
A chilling wind; grey battlements of cloud
Rimmed with gold, pale shafts of hidden fire

Fanwise to the west.
       Eight thirty-three.

A queue for hot dogs; skittish children; prams;
A roped-off bonfire darting orange flames
This way and that, on cold upswirling air.
The minutes tick away. We wait, unsure.

For we were young: what grief was this of ours?
A rumour from beyond the sky, a shadow
That fled before our childhood. Fifty years
Is long for men, in life and memory.
Yet we knew names; we saw the sad closed faces.
Their grief has been our freedom.
              A maroon
Cracks like a whip. A deep obedient hush
Falls on the hill; coats rustle; one small child
Cries and is rocked. We stand. Two minutes pass.
Mist on the plain beneath, a white half-moon
Strengthening above.
       Then bugle notes,
A roll of drums. The solemn statues move,
Speak and are ordinary. We go back,
Torches aloft; cars nose the narrow lane.
Something is served: at least, our silence said
All that the living can say to the dead.

JANUARY NIGHT

Black wind from the north. A pewter moon
Gleams on wet roads.

Pits of the year. Christmas two weeks gone
And cinder-cold.

The sleet wind sands my eyes. My knuckles sting.

And now the lion hill,
Bellowing, black-maned,
A farmstead in its paws.

I run as I have run
These forty years tonight.

What's courage? Glycogen,
Food in the belly, warmth.

No, that's the body's courage. When that runs out? My dear,
You don't have long.
          Black clouds
Smoke across the moon.
The spirit's candle gutters,
Steadies itself. Then why?

Something to remember,
A scrip, a talisman,
Against the dreams of loss.

The hill's long scorching labour
Ends; the moon comes clear.

Or shall we say: a binding,
For such nights too are bridal:
Their covenant endures.

Do you take this earth,
This body and this life?

Downhill my footfalls hammer:
I do. I do. I do.

AMNIO

As the needle pierced the taut drum of the stomach
And slid on its sampling way, I who was watching
With never a thought of blench felt suddenly
A shock, a sharp electric jolt, that had me
Head over knees, uniting wife and nurse
In a tart solidarity: useless bloody men ... .

And that was unjust to a veteran of the birth-room
Who five months on would watch with only wonder
The Caesar's open sesame, my daughter
Lifted into life through the door of flesh
Perfect, but for, on her chest, one blemish
Like the healed, expanded scar of a needle's prick.

Who, knowing the lies and postures of the trade,
Would trust a poet's tale? I am not given
To credit this myself. Some psychic bond?
But loved ones disappear from us each day

Or suffer worse than pinpricks in darkened rooms,
And what do we know, till the knock, the phone-call comes?

Nonetheless, it happened. I revisit
This awkward nugget of the irrational.
Imagination's mere coincidence?
My wife admits: yes, at the time I claim
The baby jerked. But did it help to faint?
A woman for you, sharp and to the point.

DAUGHTER, AGED FIVE

I drop you off at school on the way to work.
You rush into the classroom, then rush back
For one more cuddle. 'Wave to me through the window!'
I see your small face watching as I go.

Frost on the grass; a white sky; nothing here
Time has not brought uncounted times before,
And so the mornings of the world go by.
What shall we have, a thousand, you and I

To share like this? Back at the car I feel
My face still foolish with love's parting smile,
And frown, too late repairing a defence
Long swept away by trust and innocence.

THE VISITORS

They come like birds of passage now, alighting
To spend the night, not often more; they bring
Girl-friends, babies, gossip, sprawl. The house
Becomes a tidal pool: it fills and empties
While I, unsettled vaguely by that flow,
Patrol my shore, and watch them come and go.

There should be things to say, but what they are
I never quite decide. Should I inquire
After their deepest lives, ask: are you happy?
If they are not, what help now is in me?
So I withdraw from such impertinence
To small talk, or companionable silence.

What could I say to them? Mistrust the glamour
Of unfulfilment: if there is no more
Let things be simple, find your happiness
In gratitude that there should be no less,
Though this, as yet, they would not understand
Who come as migrants now, to foreign land.

NO ANSWER

Grandad, what was it like? Why, it was like
Being young is always: vivid, cruel,
Muddled, ecstatic ... should I simply say
It was all a long time ago and I do not remember?
Oh, but I do: we batten down our days

Like a slave-ship's cargo: lift the hatch and there
Huddled incomprehensions stir, a hold
Of human baggage reeks like Africa.

For if the teens were my Renaissance, these
Were my Dark Ages: rank, unchronicled.
My mother was ill and went away; the trains
Made a lonely sound at night; I feared the dark
And had no lamp. Yes, there was kindness too:
But what endures? A brass tap in a playground,
The smell of chalk and milk-crates, rainy mornings,
The tick of boredom, old barbarities.

The grown-up have few choices, but the young
Have none at all: their facts lie all around
But point to nowhere yet, like iron filings
Unmarshalled by the magnet of their power.
Must I explore them then, those unmapped years,
My last white spaces, where the dragons are?
This is no answer, nor yet history:
I have not done with this, nor this with me.

EARTH TO EARTH

Forgive me, most faithful lover, I know you're still making
Gifts to me: today in the meadow it was
A burnet moth in its magician's cloak
Of black and crimson; last night, broken cloud
Around a full moon, rainbowed with its burnish.
Forgive me, then, if I seem to look away
Like one embarrassed by what he cannot repay.

If I said that I was tired, would you understand,
You who never grow tired, whose poems unfold
In the soft thick parchment of magnolia petals,
A guaranteed perfection, old as spring?
You have suffered too, but to be a creature divided
Against itself is a thing you have not known.
For you, all's oneness: water, sunlight, stone.

What my own kind want of me, you would understand,
Knowing their ways, to covet, to consume.
They plough the field of my mind, they harrow me
With sharp needs, make their urgent sowings, reap
Their profitable harvests. But you would have me
Only alert, and fallow, listening
In a dry country for the hidden spring.

Once it was easy to return to you:
When I ran like a fox, and the hunt of the world went by
As I lay in your arms, in the breath of summer bracken.
I loved to run at dusk on grass, barefoot,
Palping the planet, till I dropped and lay
Immortal, melded, watching blue air swim,
Feeling the blood bliss throb in every limb.

Those paths close up, or we abandon them.
Need narrows us, till all our ways are one,
But that leads back: bear with me as I bear,
Holding myself still upright, as I must,
Against your green embrace, your gravity.
As fox to earth at last, to grass the dew,
As love to lover, I shall come to you.

SUCCESS

In this overcrowded island
Our lives are like land

And people want them so.
They have crops to grow,

Roads to make, buildings to raise.
So you sell them your days.

It is prison to be poor.
But they want more

Asking 'And what about those
Deep hours like meadows,

Those long days left to lie
For ragwort and butterfly?'

And they come, not once or twice,
Each time with a higher price

As if your stubborn freehold
Were mocking at their gold.

How pleased they are, if you sell.
They call it doing well.

But you, when you contemplate
Time's vanishing estate,

Will you rue the bargains you made?
For this is one-way trade:

Do not think to buy them back,
Those acres that you lack.

LUCRE

The river of money has nothing to do with me.
It rises somewhere in the mysterious catchments
Of corporations; debouches, passing me by,
In a broad consumer sea; ascends again
To fall on those rich hinterlands like rain.

How blessed are its waters, which endow
Mortgage companies, missiles, minor royals.
Why have I never knelt in reverence
Beside that trustable transmuting flow?
Indeed, I have heard its voice, seductive, low:

'Not for yourself then: for the desert lives
That you could irrigate, the parching needs
You might have slaked ... .' And I regret their loss
And mine, or would, but for another voice
That mocks, and cherishes, and leaves no choice.

THE SLEEPER

The story is: two centuries ago
A girl from one of these lost villages
Fell asleep, and slept for twenty years,

As if she sailed a boat out into mist
And floated there, her vacant body tended
(A heart-wrung mother), till one day she woke;

Was hungry; ate some soup; endured brief wonder;
Married, and never leaving shore again
Lived out a steady, uneventful span.

Where did she go? The living must be somewhere.
I am haunted by the dark fields of her sleep,
Her loosened spirit falling like fine rain

On moss and chalk, an unseen visitor
Returning to old borders, lightly drawn
As hawfinches to hornbeam-tops in spring.

I cannot tell why I should brood this so,
Probing a long-scabbed, legendary hurt,
As if for meaning: why should there be meaning?

I cannot even, at the last, be sure
What more disturbs me: whether that great loss
And childless blank of sleep, or else her waking

To ordinariness, to reabsorption:
An uninvolved contentment's perfect coma,
Until, somewhere, she slept, or woke, again.

ENDANGERED SPECIES

Words too, though these live on, after a fashion,
When the things that they were meant for cease to be:
Names of old flowers, coins, breeds of cattle,
The jargons of forgotten crafts and trades,
Lost argots from the rookeries of language,
Or simply shades, discriminations, caught
In uniformity's extinctions: these
Survive, but in a kind of widowhood,

Like a valley that has lost its stream: the mill,
The settlement are gone; no-one comes now
Riffling the dead leaves of a sunken bed
But lexicographers, unless some poet,
His vagrant step drawn to the ghost of water,
Stops beside the dry course, noticing
A clump of jewelweed, a polished pebble
Where once the sunlit meanings flashed and sang.

LIMESTONE PAVEMENT

The sunlit, swarming, coccolithic sea.
What myriads are here, what memory.

Seas drain away, to leave a gleaming skin.
A writing-block. The pens of time begin.

Ice. The stiff stone flexes; eased again,
Cracks and crazes like fine porcelain.

The purest rain is acid. Rocks decay
Where runnelled waters etch the jointed way.

Scribed by that slow calligrapher, each age
Lies lettered on this legendary page.

Sun glitters on the folios of lime
But black with shadow are the runes of time.

Somewhere deep, a murmur like the sea.
What myriads are here, what memory.

THE LOST WEATHERS

What was it like, the day that Caesar came?
Autumn, they say: a sharp rain on the sea,
The gold woods hissing like a sodden fire?
On Senlac Hill, I wonder: did the sun
Burn through a mist at morning, or did only
Impartial, imperturbable grey cloud
Soak up the song of Taillefer, the grunt
Of Harold's axe-men, 'Ut, ut!', round their lord.

Climate has archaeologies: we raise
Summers from peat and pollen, conjure rains
From thicknesses of tree-ring, lakes of thaw
From layered silt. Weather's another thing,
Irrevocable, wind and cloud, the day's
Unique unnoted slant of light: I mourn
Those lost particularities, that flesh
Long vanished from the bones of our occurrence.

How shall the past be real, unless we know
What shade the rocks cast at Thermopylae,
What scent the sea winds had that came to Troy?
And there are other things I have desired:
The first rains of the earth, falling like seas,
The hot plains and the stink of dinosaurs,
The blue returning northward springs that broke
The brutal age-long hammerlock of Ice.

Vast interwoven energies, and we
Pick out one thread, and call it history ...
I think the earth remembers otherwise:
An almanac of lost celestials
In whose defining elemental light
We show proportioned, marginal, as we
Might note the weather: rain at midnight, clearing,
Or broken cloud, soon giving way to sun.

THE GOOD OLD DAYS

I'll tell you this, the good old days were cold.
November through to March, our fire was lit
Mid-afternoon, burned up to warmth by evening
When you could get at it for drying clothes
And when it hadn't been put out by falls
Of soot or snow, or else my father burning
Shovelfuls of frozen nutty slack
Scraped from the backyard bunker, or wet logs.

The wind would moan and rattle in the hall.
Doing my homework, six feet from the fire,
I'd freeze on one side, scorch upon the other
Like one of Dante's sinners. Sunday night
Was bath night; being youngest, I came last
To tepid greasy water heated up
With kettles, while our ancient oil-stove fluttered
Moth-wings of warmth against the icy air.

Going to bed, you shivered for ten minutes
In crackling sheets, curled up your feet away
From arctic nether regions, tried again
And then it came, a warmth at last, like none
A coddled generation can imagine,
A Stone Age bliss, a blood-heat; so you slept,
Waking to winter harvest: sheaves of frost
Heraldic, radiant, on every pane.

NJAL

Why did Njal unleash his terrible sons?
There have been more pitiable stories, but few so stark.
How shall a man do good, if this one failed
Who wanted peace, who said that only laws
Can build the land that lawlessness lays waste?

The tale is complex: hard now to unpick
The hurts and hatreds, woven so far back.
The feud was like a fire in heather roots
That smouldered on beneath his stamping feet
And crept by hidden paths to flare again.

So Gunnar died, whom Njal had tried to save,
A leaping salmon, taken in doom's net:
'I never saw the fields more fair', he said,
'With corn and new-mown grass; I will not go'
And turned for home, preferring death to exile.
Was it then the heart went out of Njal?

Watch him like a dancer, desperate
For reason and alliance in a world
Where men move like locked wheels that cannot leave
The bloody ruts of retribution's road.

His enemies made mock of him, and this
He would have borne, but there were other things:
The honour of a wife, his chafing sons
Like stags in velvet. So the sons went forth.

Evil will come, said Njal, and evil came:
Blood, and more death, and Njal in the burning house
Saw no escape but one from honour's code
And took an oxhide and lay down beneath
To die in calm abstention or atonement,
As his sons fought on, and his enemies closed round.

Those with no part in the feud they allowed to go,
Being after their fashion honourable men,
And Flosi their leader pleaded with Bergthora,
In no circumstances wishing to harm a woman,
But she answered: 'I was given young to Njal.
We shall not be parted now.' And the little grandson
Chose to stay also, and they lay down with him.

A thousand years, yet truth is in the detail.
When the kinsmen come at morning, what will they find

But the great axe, driven deep into the woodwork,
Where a tall son burned, and the old ones side by side
With the child between, intact but for a finger
Where the hide had not quite covered one small hand.

So, these things happened. Where is Njal's victory?
That we should know of them, that of all sagas
The greatest bears no king's or fighter's name
But his alone, the necessary man,
Who reckoned his time's odds, and went against them:
Who knew that nothing changes but by choosing,
And nothing maybe even then, but chose.

THE GOOD WORDS

If they come less easily, the good words now,
Courage, honour, even love, is it because
We have worn them out with too much make-believe
Or because at last we understand them, how
They bind us to themselves: say 'generous'
And you must give; 'pity' and you must grieve.
Say 'courage', and endure. Always the deed
Proves, or reproves, till we learn husbandry:
Never to use those hoarded words unless
To follow where they lead, finding instead
Virtue enough in sheer necessity.
Yet still the heart remembers 'hope' and 'bless'
And lifts to them, as to a flight of birds
Bound somewhere else, beyond all deeds, all words.

THE BIRTH OF POEMS

How anonymous, how uncircumstanced are their births.
One forgets they even happened, that at some point
In the workaday time of the world, clouds going by,
Hens in the yard, dogs barking, smoke on the wind,
There had to be a mothering, a making
Of words unmade: 'No longer mourn for me',
'Ah no, the years, the years!', 'Western wind,
When wilt thou blow?', 'So I did sit and eat'.

Yes, one is curious, but they are private
As births should be, hidden beyond recall
In the hollow places of time, in the folds of its silence,
Those lost hours, when the landscape of our love
Stayed as it was for a while: when clouds went by,
Hens scratched, dogs barked, and no-one knew at all,
Except for one who sat, his own sole witness,
Smiling at blank-eyed, inattentive air.

MUSEUM PIECE

Not Kensington, this one-room cave of wonder:
I grant you that. Yet where else might you see
Item: a raven's nest, one anaconda
(Stuffed), five Dyak arrows (courtesy
Some late lieutenant-colonel), cannonballs,
A louis d'or, a German silver dollar,
The shin-bone of an ostrich, minerals
(Peacock ore, moss agate, chrysocolla),

An Aztec mask, a curling photograph,
(Young faces, sepia'ed: the Silver Band
In nineteen-twelve), the skin of a giraffe,
And in one corner, quietly to hand,
Item: a proud curator, who's not heard
This world is anything that need make sense,
But sits, contented as a bower-bird,
Selling: 'Museums: Handmaidens of Science'?
Nor is this all: beneath a print, 'The Moon,
Lake Chad', is framed an infant script, addressed
To Mr Bob: 'I liked my afternoon.
I liked it all. I liked the big snake best.'

THE BIRDS

We take it for granted: of course they will always be there
As they always have been, one of those small pivots
Our true lives turn upon, the trustable
Recurrences: I speak of the thrush at twilight,
The robin, the twig-bearing rook, the yellowhammer
Molten on the fence-post at sunset,
The finches clustered on the winter tree
Like red-gold apples: could a time truly come
When the lark did not rise from the green field by the river,
The corn-bunting jangle from wires by the windy crossroad?

Their flight weaves in and out of history
But their time is not ours: there is no mist upon
Their being's bright unalterable lens.
They are like poetry: we come back to them
After years of soil and neglect, as if they needed

No space at all, as if we had only to kneel
For their soaring, perfect, uninvolved absolution
To be bestowed on us. Well, it may be so.
Spring, and the larks are back; the sky, grown rich,
Reverberates around their vanishing.

DOLPHIN-WATCHING
for Matthew

Binoculars cut off the sky and tilt
The green sea like a page; I sit and stare
Watching as if for meaning to appear.
'There!' you say, but it's too hard for me:
The uncoordinated sea yields only
Patches of peacock blue, of wandering turquoise,
Cliff-shadow, cloud-shadow, shoal-shadow; nothing that stays.
If only, you say, we had come on some calm evening:
Then in a mirror sea the dolphins barrel,
Leaping in sport. You want me so to see them.
I look again. Was that a fin, that curve?
Nothing for sure. We give up, take the path
Above the high cliffs in the summer wind.
You honour with their names the near at hand:
Purple moor-grass, vetch, the sprinkled gold
Of lady's bedstraw, sea-blue stars of squill.
I taught you once, a little: now you know
Far more than I did then, and I have been
Too much apart from this: I had forgotten
Even the small brown gatekeeper, that lover
Of warm light and the lilac bramble-flower.
No, I could teach you nothing now, unless

A never-disappointedness, to fill
So many days between the dolphin days:
A fallback from the rare miraculous
To earth, and sky, and sunlight on the gorse.

REJECTS

You can see them now quite clearly:
    The failures of craft, of truth,
And mourn for them, as for relationships
You marred by haste, by impercipience,
    In the carelessness of youth.

And now, could you not put them right,
    Knowing what at last you know,
Not to talk, but to listen, not reach out,
But watch and wait, catching the fall of light
    In your cupped hands? Let them go:

These are not for mending, ever.
    Their voices will not return.
Your fingers, feeling for a pulse, encounter
Mist, cold glass; now let only their silence
    Remain; what it taught you, learn.

REMEMBERING THE PICNIC

There was a place, I think, a downland slope
Like a green rooftop, tilted to the sky.
I ran and fell and someone picked me up.
A voice was there, telling me not to cry.
We came back home (but I have lost the way)
On chalky paths through fields of moonlit hay.

This happened long ago and too much since.
Was it a dream, or is it memory?
I cannot tell. Is this how age begins:
A haze, unnoticed, far out on the sea,
But when you look again what's land, what's cloud?
We trust our minds. This cannot be allowed.

Listen, and wait. Somewhere within our silence,
Are guardians that falsehood may not pass:
If this was real my nose shall prick with hay-scents
And on my palms green stigmata of grass
Will burn again and blossom: I shall walk
On paths of moonlight, solid as the chalk.

THE PLANET HAPPINESS

If ever you come to the planet Happiness
You may find it resembles an old-fashioned bathing resort
With gulls and a floral clock, and a small child standing
Ankle-deep in light at the edge of the sea
Thinking of nothing at all but the drag and tickle
Of tide-drawn sand through the pudge and squirm of its toes.

Yet quickly that place can change: you may find yourself
On a mountain ridge in summer, looking down
Through calm air at the charcoal gloss of ravens
Gliding below, while a white cloud at your feet
Bumps like a boat along the precipice,
Inviting you to board. But if you do,

You must not be surprised to find yourself in a train
Travelling home through lamplit autumn dusk
With a sleeping infant heavy on your lap,
Warm as a roasted chestnut, and a woman
Smiling to see. But the train may go into a tunnel
And never come out again, leaving you wherever:

Alone, perhaps, on your own sober earth
With nothing in your pocket but some pebbles
That can never lead back, and yet, if polished smooth
By memory's long fingering, might serve
For something lost: wet sand, or summer cloud,
Or the hardness of love, on the planet Happiness.

CV

To have a craft, and not the one you'd choose,
    Is better than begging or starving.
It leaves room, even, for a certain pride:
Look, I laboured too, I paid my dues,
And earned an honest, unbeholden living.
    Ask those I worked beside.

Oh yes, we knew him. Strange chap, will they say,
  Decent enough, the conscientious sort.
His trademark was a truth, an unpretence,
But with it such a graceless, throwaway
Self-distancing from all, as if he thought
  Nothing much here made sense.

Not what you'd call a corporation man:
  Pride, yes, but no ambition, no desire.
What did he want? Like us, he said, to live.
Where did it lead? To end as he began:
A hireling, who had too much not for hire,
  Or no hire we could give.

THE REFUSAL

We get what we pay for: the big cheques that I wrote
On the credit of my days were never to Art.
That was always more a matter of time's loose change
Shelled out in passing to a patient-eyed
Collector of alms, some watchful, dispossessed
Ironic exile from eternity.

And even that sparse charity, those coins
Tossed in the echoing can, seemed more sometimes
Than prudence urged, or honour could afford,
To so much else must love stand guarantor.
What did I mean then, by that uncommitted
Careful largesse, those tithelings of the heart?

I wanted all debts paid, but life allows
Only the choice: which will you settle first?
I chose the human debt; those patient eyes
Looked to the next, as they must always do,
Seeking the rare ones, ready to endure
The long arrears of art, and exile's road.

RETIREMENT

Those final years at work:
Like almost drowning,
Which I indeed once did.

Suddenly out of your depth
You find yourself in currents
You can no longer master.

A salt, uncaring sea
Cuffs the strength from your body
And yet, the shore is near.

No, you cannot cry out.
The code of competence
Owns to no need. Sheer anger

Locks your toe at last
To shifting shoal-bank gravel.
You lurch through water, lie,

Spent, at the edge of things,
Spewing up forty years,
Till sunwarmth on your back

Kindles cold flesh; you stir
In core-deep, uncontracted
Wonderment: what now?

ONE COUNTRY

My trade diminishes as yours increases:
I am no nearer to your effortless
Colloquy with the stranger in the train,
To mastering the graceful word that eases
Or the kind word that takes away pain.

I ply my trade by patient circumspection,
Watching for when the soul's door is ajar
And I can slip through like a thief to steal,
But you are welcome there by invitation
Because you go only to give and heal.

Should I resent it then, envy a little
The gift you have I lack and so desire?
Indeed, I could have wished a change of place,
Offered all things to which my craft gives title
For your unstudied, artless human grace.

No, I am only grateful that we form
One country: love knew well then what it did,

Marrying green coast and desert sand,
Your ports of call, your trading posts of welcome,
My watchful, brooding, silent hinterland.

NOVICES

Such novices we were: what did we know
To marry, to begin a life, start lives?
We had ten pounds between us. Did it matter?
There was love, and for me in those days always a poem
Like a pebble in the pocket, waiting its time
To be taken out again for the slow caressing
Of the mind's thumb, wearing it smooth.
                    But what of you:
If I had this, what was it others had
At the rest-point of the mind, the secret place
Where no-one else can come?
                    It took so long
To understand these things, but watching you
Apprenticed to your own grave crafts of care,
First teacher, mother next, at last I saw
Who kept the centre for me.
                    And did you
Imagine, for these middle years, your art
Grown effortless, a mastery complete
And never to be lost? They do, the young.
But lovers, parents and poets are always apprentices.
How could that learning end? Now you begin
Again: the grandchild on your lap, and I
Feel something rough against my callused thumb.

from

NEW AND SELECTED POEMS

(2005)

THE PROGRAMMER'S TALE

The mountain men came first: von Neumann, Turing,
Mapping the country, then the pioneers
Following their westward trail; call us
The cowboys then: we lived a brief wild era,
Riders of the electronic range,
Drifters, oddball unemployables,
Coming together on the raw new ranches,
Driving the code-herds up to Abilene.

What was it like? What history is like
For those that live it: sweat and toil, redeemed
By rude self-mocking camaraderie.
No-one, I think, will make a myth of us:
Our skills were real enough, but unheroic,
A kind of naked wit: in languages
Forgotten now as cuneiform we penned
A shadow poetry of pure precision.

And did we see it, what was going on?
A few, not me: for my kind there was only,
Myopic and intense, the task at hand.
An esoteric humdrum owned our lives:
Blizzards of the immediate, dust-storms, droughts.
The bones of abandoned projects whitened the prairies
And yet the job was done: for pride and pay
We built the cyber-world. And then it ended:

The range was fenced, time and the market tamed
Our bright irreverence: we found ourselves
Outlandish among children, old-timers
With campfire stories from another world.

Well, we had had our turn at being young.
Quietly, one by one, we slipped away
Down faded trails, seeking remembered valleys,
The lost, eroded landscapes of the real.

A CANDLE FOR MR SOKOLOWSKI

Mr Sokolowski cut hair
In a one-room shop, with till and toiletries,
Chairs and a tall bright mirror. This lit cave
Was Mr Sokolowski's life, this floor
He cleared of its soft sweepings, endlessly,
And these still heads, like heads in prayer, that he
Addressed so fluently, with flashing scissors
And barber's talk, like candle-ends, relit
Smilingly for each new customer:
The match on Saturday, children, the weather.

Who was Mr Sokolowski? Once
A customer spoke of his fussy child:
'Eats nothing.' Mr Sokolowski's eyes
Altered then, I saw it in the mirror.
'You get hungry, eat damn anything.
Ate rat in Russia. Some, worse thing than rat.'
Snip. Snip, snip. The customer's reflection
Nods a surprised and meaningless agreement
And Mr Sokolowski smiles once more:
'So, what you think for game on Saturday?'

Mr Sokolowski shut up shop
Years ago; retired; some seaside place.
Must be dead now: even survivors die
To dream no more of cutting hair, the weather,
The match on Saturday, or other things.

EMBASSY

It looms like war, this growing old: we live
    On new frugalities of expectation.
The provident have sold up and are gone
    Like refugees from truth's beleaguered nation.
Lady, shall we grow circumspect at last
    And close the embassy of adoration?

The years are baying like a Boxer mob
    And soon enough their pillaging must start.
The documents are all secured, or burned.
    What duty now forbids us to depart
That still we stay, the tattered flag of love
    Unstruck above the refuge of the heart?

HEROIC IDEAL

'Hige sceal þe heardra, heorte þe cenre,
mod sceal þe mare, þe ure mægen lytlað.'
– The Battle of Maldon

I bet those words were never said at all,
At least not that way. In the thick of battle,
Lead-limbed, parched of lung, swinging a sword
On wet ground treacherous with guts and blood,
A sea of nightmare faces howling hatred,
Your mates decamping, all your leaders dead,
You're likely, right, to spout bravura verse
Polished enough to last a thousand years?
'Let spirits now be harder, hearts be keener,
Let courage be the more as we grow weaker' –
Some Saxon Churchill, then: good leader-work
Dubbed on defeated lips: this was Dunkirk
Without deliverance: we ran and died.
No wonder, then, we looked so hard for pride.

But this I might believe, that in the fight
Some bonehead, unaware of history's spotlight,
Seeing that he had come to the end of his luck,
Muttered the Anglo-Saxon for 'Oh fuck'
And then, among the fleeing, stood his ground.
Whatever. True or not, the words resound,
Unironical, accusing, tough:
Saying not everything, and yet enough.

BEYOND

Beyond the god of pure intelligence
Who can calculate, for example, in zero time,
Whether any zillion-digit number is prime
    Stands the god of pure existence
Who does not calculate at all, but knows,
Being in the numbers as in the unfolding rose.

Beyond the god of multiplicity
Who takes for worship all that is defined
By the forever pluralising mind
    Stands the god of unity
Who says that sun is rose, and rose is sun,
Who is all primes eternally, and One.

JOURNAL

I write in my journal, 'Thrushes in the lane,
A soft wind, and the blackthorn petals falling.'
There would have been much more when I was young:
Each scent of earth, each bird and flower of spring,
But youth is gone, I cannot visit again
The adventure of the blackbird's first song.

And once, I might have wanted to share such words
But now it seems enough that they are for me,
And in time, if time allows, will quicken this day,
Since love, in the end, needs little for memory,
But makes of petals, soft winds, singing birds,
Its momentary, everlasting stay.

COSMOLOGIES

'If you could just keep going in a straight line' –
Said my father, innocent of Einstein,
As we walked home one night of winter stars –
'You'd come at last to somewhere where there was
Nothing at all. I mean, there has to be
A last star, and what then?' This troubled me.
That night in bed I travelled in my mind
Through stars that whirled like snowflakes in the wind
Until I found, beyond one last faint glow,
A blank, like morning fog outside my window.
I woke and cried, but when my father came
To ask what ailed me, was it some old dream,
Sobbed 'Nothing!', so was left to sleep again
Like the blind Cyclops in his cave of pain.

Later I learned: my father had it wrong:
All lines bend back at last, however long.
There is no end to the great blizzard of light
I'd like to tell him now, and so I might
Had he not journeyed on, to somewhere far
Beyond all words of mine, and any star.

SIXTY

The dreams of women do not end, but now
All's gentleness: the brushing of bare arms,
A look, the touch of fingers. Strange then, how
If passion's gone I wake out of these dreams

Throbbing with an anguish of desire
Even my youth did not know. A feather's touch
Might lacerate, my body burns like fire.
I cannot sleep again, not after such
Disquietude; I go downstairs, make tea,
Then, as another dawn whitens the garden,
Sit with familiar poets suddenly
Electric, comforting myself with pain,
Caressing words of loss, keener than knives,
Holding ungloved the bright wire of their lives.

IMMIGRANTS

Where did they come from? From so many lands.
From mountains, jungles, deserts, snowy plains,
From regions of hot grass, from great slow rivers.
I think there was no country upon earth
That did not send these secret embassies.

Turquoise. Apricot. Mahogany.

How did they get here? In so many ways.
They came in peace and war, with song and story:
Marching in with dusty, sunburnt soldiers;
By caravan along the Silk Road; borne
In white-sailed clippers; carried on the spice wind.
None checked their coming here; no customhouse
Could hinder these that travelled light as air.

Maharajah. Sandal. Talisman.

And did we make them welcome? They were seed.
We gave them earth: some withered, some took root.
At first they tingled on our tongue, like snowflakes,
But then the strangeness melted: they were ours.

Typhoon. Anaconda. Kangaroo.

And will they come again? Never like that.
A language also has its innocence,
Its first fine careless hospitality.
Never again so multitudinous
Those migrants to our shore, like unknown birds
Alighting for the first time, opening
The proud fan of their peacock syllables.

Oleander. Lilac. Cinnamon.

THE CRAFTSMEN

In the country of the one-eyed I was blind.
I see it now: I was not good at things,
Or not at things that mattered to my people.
My mind could get no purchase on machines,
My fingers were not apt for tool or brush.
I failed all boyhood's tests: balsa, meccano,
Could offer nothing but a dumb ox strength.
I fetched and carried, glad to be of use.

My craftsmen tribe all but despaired of me,
Decorators, plumbers, carpenters,

Canny and proud, boasting their graduation
From life's university, the school of hard knocks.
They ribbed me for my reading, kind but sharp,
As for some Galilean heresy:
They knew with geocentric certainty
Nothing worth learning ever came from books.

Fifty years on, I hear their accusations
Unanswered still, unanswerable now.
Truly, I bear no rancour: this long quarrel
Is with myself, not them, with my own stubborn,
Impractical, unprofitable craft.
I wonder, though: what if it had been music?
They liked a tune … we might have met in music,
Or so I tell myself, in unshared words.

THE HOUSE

Come and live, they said,
In the house of science
With its solid floor of sense,
Its tiled and timbered roof,
Its foursquare walls of proof.

But I chose instead
The house of poetry
Under its rowan tree,
Half ruin and half grave
With green grass like a wave,

Nettles and moss for bed,
And its people coming and going
Like seeds the wind might bring,
Like words in the wind's song,
Their tenancy not long.

THE WOODS

The woods near my house are strange.
On the map, a few square miles
Penned between road and river.
It should not be possible
To walk all day in April
Through layers of leaf and birdsong
Nor to drift through the long hours
Of summer twilight (outside
Bright fields still giving back
The barley breath of noon)
Yet meet neither road nor person.

And I think of that other wood
Which occupies so few acres
In the country of my life
Yet endures in its own time
And strange geometry,
Where too the familiar paths
Are never quite as remembered
In the shifting dapple of light
As they lead to that adventure
Which is after all only the known's
Illimitable surprise.

TO AIR

It seems too light a sound
For this invisible benevolence,
This unpraised necessity, like married love,
That makes all things possible.

Better than any wine
Are your vintages to me:
The coolness that distils
In the honeysuckled hollows
Of summer lanes at midnight,
The grey, stone-scented air
Of winter churches at dusk
And the prickle of salt mist
From quiet seas like silk.
I watch by autumn fields
As the plough turns up my childhood
Sharp with raw earth and smoke.

Giver, protector, who tames
Our star's fierce golden furnace
To a whisper of perfect warmth,

Amenable medium,
In whom the ripples of our loneliness
Reach out and meet, in whose domain we build
Our vibrant habitations, music, words,

It is wrong, that litany
That wills us to the grave. The best of us
Does truly go elsewhere.
Think how we hear them, how we shape them still

Over and over, the lost beloved voices
Shelved in your secret libraries. And listen,
That note you always hold, that undersong
Even in silence: earth to earth, it says,
But air to air.

AT STEEP
for Myfanwy Thomas on her 90th birthday

Driving home through Hampshire with my daughter
I see a sign that beckons like a legend
Though on plain earth, and so it is we come
In April twilight, clearing after rain,
Like pilgrim ghosts your childhood might have seen
Out of its unimaginable future,
Up Stoner Hill and round by Cockshott Lane,
To find, through trees and down a root-stepped path,
Your father's boulder, set there on the slope.

My daughter runs ahead of me, downhill
Past dim white cherries, cowslips, violets,
Mildly curious, but wanting tea.

'Who was Edward Thomas anyway?'
I say 'A poet.' 'Oh.' My daughter's twelve,
Likes judo, dancing, being with her friends.
Poems are the things that daft Dads write
Light-years away from coolness.
            'Was he good?'
So short a question. And so long an answer
If truth were served: as long, say, as long years

Of looking, loving, waiting.
          'He was good.'

I take her photograph beside the stone.
'Can we go back now?' Yes, my love, we can.
To keep the covenant was all I wanted.
You see, this is our obscure faith, our trust,
Whether we live or die too soon, unknowing,
That somewhere in the private rooms of time
Others will read for love alone the words
We wrote for love, alone.
          And deeper still
There is another covenant we keep:
Let our words be forgotten, let our lives
Fade utterly, but not these: let there be
Always an April evening, woods, a thrush
Singing and a child, always a child,
A daughter, maybe, finding violets
Or standing in the twilight by a path,
Plucking a bush, with one to see her there
Apart, in all a child's grave otherness,
And love her.
          'Can we get chips?' We get chips.

from

NO THROUGH ROAD

(2013)

NO THROUGH ROAD

What was it like, retiring? It was like
Stepping off a main road suddenly,
Leaving behind the haze of oil and dirt,
The rush and suck of cars, and finding yourself
Back in some half-remembered country lane
Leading unhurriedly up into hills.

You let the healing quietness enfold you.
So little traffic here, the strip you tread
Is velveted with moss, the brush of grass
Caresses you. Slowly the names come back:
Teasel, tall mullein, toadflax, surfacing
From days so deep you thought them lost forever.

It does not seem to matter overmuch
That in all probability this lane leads nowhere:
That sooner or later there will be no farm
In the hidden fold of the hill, no dung-starred gateway,
That the grass-grown tarmac will peter out altogether
In a path that is lost in the deepening shadow of trees.

For now at least it seems enough to walk
As in some end of summer afternoon,
The harvest done, the sky milky with cirrus,
Rooks feeding in the fields – enough to heal
From labour's long irrelevance; perhaps
From servitude set free, at last to serve.

THE CRAFT

No, it is not science, we cannot say
I will do this, and this, and this will happen
Though science may image its process well enough
In the shudder of the final crystal that seeds
The saturated, long-prepared solution.

Nor is it magic: spirits there may be
But they will not come for pentagram or circle
Yet may appear, unlooked-for and unbidden,
In the supermarket queue, or as we drive
Absently down some familiar street.

What then is left, to underwrite this craft?
Only the human weave, the love and loss
And waiting, for what may or may not come
From some cold reach of time to warm itself
At the flame of an inexplicable devotion.

ACCEPTANCE

We stop at the garden centre for tea and cake,
Our time our own now, all the children gone,
And you talk to another couple at the next table
While I half-drowse in late October sun,
Answering your smiles on cue, but thinking
This is not me, not yet, or not today:
I am not ready for the small contentments,
Though what I want instead is hard to say.

Our forty years again, of toil and trial?
Indeed, if strength came with them to endure
All that love asks, the given and the taken,
But we have come where only loss is sure,
So I must learn new lines, an awkward actor
Who thought to have no part in age's play.
Rehearse me, then, in love's last role, acceptance.
Above all, till the final curtain, stay.

FIRST NIGHT

I like to think of when your words were new
And came like scalding lava, before they cooled
Into a long familiar fantastic
Or to try, like you, always another image,
Of that long summer when our language bloomed
And you went stumbling like a drunken bee
From wayside herb to blossom-laden bough –
Never such harvest, nor such honeycomb.

But most I like to think of that first night,
The crowd spilling out, to walk by the starlit river
Full of it all: the ghost, the poor drowned girl,
The sword-fight at the end, and quoting lines
That smouldered on, like coals in thatch: and then
That bit about the undiscover'd country,
How did it go, To be or not to be?
Neat, anyway; you've got to give him that.

RTFP

Just an RTFM, support would say,
Putting the phone down, fifty times a day,
On customers who simply would not look
At clear instructions in a printed book
So got themselves in some unholy mess.
It stood for 'Read The Manual', more or less ...
Why did they find it difficult, we sighed,
To do their bit, when we had really tried,
Or so we claimed, to render things as plain
As anything can be from brain to brain.

Of course, the customer is right: he pays.
Yet shouldn't poets too have such a phrase
For readers who'll do anything but read
The words set out in front of them, who need
Critics, paraphrases, exegeses,
Even, God help us, academic theses?
I'm sympathetic, almost on their side:
I know it's hard, having no place to hide.
But that's the way it is, just you and me.
So give up now. Or else, RTFP.

BLACKTHORN DAY

A western wind, sudden and soft as May,
Long looked for yet amazing: perfect spring,
The year's first windflowers, blossom in the wood,
The new air tart with nettle-growth and dung.

A day like hope: how quickly we forget
The soul's long winter, when the sleet winds blew.
We surface now like dolphins into light.
To wait time out seems all we had to do.

It will not last, of course: we shall awake
To ordinary greyness and the rain.
So be it then: I would not wish a world
Unseasoned by such sweet recurring pain
Nor ask a heaven, that had no escape
From cloudless summers of eternal now
To mortal spring again, and blackthorn hope
For one day only, perfect on the bough.

PARENTS

Yes, I was impatient with your world:
Its genteel deference, its docile-tough
Pride in adversity. Was I the child
Of these poor lives, these people who knew only
How to be kind, and it was not enough?

You took me for a walk when I was small
And I ran on, over a ridge, ignoring
Your calls behind, delighted with my daring,
And found my country, solitude, green hills,
The sun at morning high and glittering
In endless air. I wanted to go on
Ridge after ridge, to world's end: how I chafed
To wait and walk in your slow company.

Your voices die behind me. My own gait
Is slower now; impatient with my world
My children have run on and look, the sun
Has all but westered. Still, I must press on:
Not all's discovered: it may even be
Just as you liked to believe, and I could not,
That love will wait for us, and all shall meet
Somewhere beyond the next ridge, or world's end.

VIRTUAL REALITY

Where will it end, do you think? With some damned scanner
Mining our brains for neural traces, lodes
Locked in the deep of memory, love-thick?
Maybe they'll build, atom by layered atom,
Such simulacra we shall weep, befooled
To see the green trees of old Earth grow back,
The swans above the river flying still,
Even the dead wife turn again and smile,
Safe in her arms the warm yet witless child.

Not in my time, I think, and it's as well.
What should I be but some last Luddite, scorning
Those resurrected unrealities,
A cyber-recusant, affecting still
My own archaic conjury of ghosts
By words on paper – think of it – mere marks
Yet potent once, men found, almost to make
The dead indeed come walking, as we knew them,
Real and unhaloed, out of eternity's sunrise.

ROOMS

Seventy draws near. My days are busy
But waking in the dawn I find myself
Alone now in the house of memory,
Trying the handles of familiar doors
    That will no longer open.

Look, here is the room of my young strength,
That smelt of summer grass, whose windows opened
On moonlit lanes, on woodland paths at sunset,
When I thought the fire of my body everlasting
    As water, earth and air.

And in this room my infant children slept.
I listen at the door: no quiet breathing
To reassure me now; within these walls
Lie only book and bear and doll, bewildered
    By long abandonment.

And this is poetry's room, that held a light
Like April, curtainless, with leaf and blossom
Astir beyond the glass. Here too I listen
As for an answer: where and how and why
    Did I lose this one's key?

Then morning comes; the ghostly house dissolves
And you are there, our long companionship
Not ended yet and now, just for a moment,
Not taken quite for granted, here in this
    Last unlocked room of love.

EXPANDING UNIVERSE

Of course, we always knew it in our heart
That the falcon stars would fly away forever,
That even gravity's great leash or lure
Could never call them back to their bright start,

For even in our own lives' little space
Worlds have departed that we could not hold,
And we have seen creation's fire grow cold
And love forever torn from our embrace.

LEAP SECOND (31/12/2008)

How curious, this chock of time we put
Under the gates of midnight swinging to.
The stars above the blank street do not change,
Earth gallops on breakneck towards the dawn
As ever, while our trusting children sleep,
Their small hands tangled in its mane of darkness.
But something is changed, the god of clocks who lives
In the dance of the caesium atom is placated,
And so it is our seasons will not drift:
We shall not plant for snow in summer, nor find
At journey's end a universe askew.
It seems we cannot wholly trust ourselves
To earth or stars, but we must engineer
The scheme of things a little, must impose,
Now and again, on their indifference
Our own impeccable coincidence.

SLIDE SHOW

Poor prisoners, trapped in one tense,
We need such arts to cut and stain
The living moments that we sense
But cannot lengthen or detain.

For you, your cunning box of light,
Your microtome that wafers time,
Whose mounted specimens tonight
Bring back the summers of our prime.

For me? Oh, I am less precise,
I lack such neat transparencies.
Rightly you chide my slow device
That yields no images like these

And yet, I claim, can work afar
To fix upon the mind's own plate
Love's moment like a shooting-star
Drawn vanishing on night's black slate.

But there's no rivalry in this:
I reverence your focussed gaze
And you, who knows, one day may miss
My convolute, archaic ways.

Tonight is yours: upon the screen
The photons of a long-set sun
Repaint our past in summer green.
What love and care can do is done.

JANUARY MORNING

Frost; a whitegold sun. Fields float on air,
Caught between haze and dazzle.
Dead oak leaves trimmed with ermine; hoofprints proud,
Rimmed with a silver sift, on crusty paths.
On dinted puddles, vertebrae of ice
X-rayed on water's blackness,

And I, in my sixty-seventh new-made year,
Thinking myself immortal for pure joy
At paddocks, red-tiled roofs, rook-visited
White corduroys of ploughland, as I walk
With warmth on one cheek, chill upon the other,
Not quite in shadow, at the woodland's edge.

RAGGLE TAGGLE

I walk half the night, then lie beneath the stars
Alone on silent downs. The summer dark
Is like an ocean shallow, warm and thick,
Laced with cool currents as the night wind stirs.

I am a carven angel, looking down,
The sky beneath, a glinting marble floor.
If earth released me, I should fall forever
Dropping like a stone down the well of dawn.

Oh, never fear, my truant heart shall turn
Soon enough to human company,

Substitute for this uncaring heaven
Love's intimate and constelled sky.

But not tonight, when stars and angels call.
Tonight I am no human thing at all.

LOGOS

A summer garden, and the scent of grass.
A hot dark flower; my sister saying 'Tulip',
And sudden understanding: speech was gift,
Was summoning. Even today the word

Shimmers in my mind; saying it now
I taste again the day's new heat, remember
The innocent delight that was no less
An end of innocence, a closing gate

With no way back to that forgotten first
World before the world grew separate:
To essence, and the nameless heart of things,
And light, cascading silently, forever.

LANGUAGE

Its maps, they say, are in our minds already:
How else could we adventure in that country
  So sure of paths we never walked upon?

I listen to the children, not yet three,
Dancing out the tongue's deep mystery,
  Threading the maze of meaning and connection.

Then what of this, this craft of poetry?
Oh, our best art is pure discovery:
  We come on what we know, beyond invention,

As if it had long waited, like a tree
Rooted in trust of time's fortuity,
  Beside the road we chanced to travel on.

THE UNFORGIVEN

My father's father's father killed himself.
Weary of staring down the double barrels
Of pain and dependence, he took a cutthroat razor
And slashed his neck. This to my father was shame.
He would not speak of it, being a child
Of old hard times that had no room for pity,
There being bread to win and wars to fight.
What of the daughter who found him, he would have said,
Who followed the trail of blood from path to door?

Poor shade, I tracked you down though, in the archive:
The clinical postmortem, drily noting
Osteoarthritis, Bright's disease,
The witness of the kind bewildered neighbour:
'He always seemed a cheery sort of chap',
And then, your daughter's words. I cannot judge.
Some lonely terror took you in plain daylight
Or was it cruel courage at the end?
Now, in this unimagined century,
Let pity rule, although your daughter's cry
Still scalds the heart: 'Oh Dad, what have you done?'

COMPROMISE

I always said, and not entirely joking,
That if a time came when I couldn't walk
Thirty miles in a day with a fifty pound rucksack
Or run ten miles in the hour at the drop of a hat,
I'd shuffle off a coil too clearly mortal.
Ah, how one compromises, year by year.

How do the great ones deal with it, reduced
To painful plodding, each a sad Achilles
Trapped in the underworld of memory?
Probably like me, by self-deception:
Just get this dodgy knee right, lose two stone,
We'll be in business, boys. Only we won't.

All the same, one has to stick around.
There is always a last endeavour, like a last poem.

One does not quit, whatever. Ah, but Samson,
You lucky man, would things have gone so well
Had you lived on to lock your arms round these
Unyielding pillars, illness and old age?

SO SOON

Are we to finish, then, with being young
So soon, when we have scarcely learned to live,
With so much to fulfil in what we might be,
In what we have been, so much to forgive?

We think that age will never come to us,
Or if it does, that with it must be sent
For all our loss an equal consolation:
Such calm and clockless hours as childhood spent,

The sun through leaves, perhaps, in a wild garden
Unknown to duty's formal, mapped estate,
Time for the random sequences of self
That care's equations could not generate,

And still, somehow, the step far-ranging, limber
As once it was, the eye undimmed, alert,
And after long confusion, understanding:
A woody healing for the young green hurt ...

All this we ask, since nothing now can answer
But fragile hope to keep us unafraid,
Like travellers across a land of winter
Who look to come upon a summer glade.

SILVA

Oak is a Tudor monarch, a big-bellied Henry
Spreading great limbs: I claim this earth, this sky.

Beech asks little space: a slender dancer,
Minding her elbows on the woodland floor.

Elm is a full-sailed galleon: alas,
Stealthy the storm that wrecked its green armadas.

Hazel is humble, yet honoured in its home
By salmon-haunted pools of secret wisdom.

Birch is all but ghost, its twigs hair-thin,
A crazing on the sky's blue porcelain.

Rowan is slight, but steadfast against evil,
Its orange lightning brilliant on the hill.

Willow strokes the stream with long cool fingers,
A green cloud in the depth of mirrored skies.

Ash is a warrior: give him no more
Than rock, an inch of soil; he will endure.

Yew alone will stand when stone has vanished,
Though nothing living sleeps in that dark shade.

RIDDLE

I am given a birth-gift: I bear a magic bag,
A carrier I keep for joy in my journey.
Behold, I stuff it with stars, I fill it with faces,
Words I winnow in, all manner of marvel,
And the bag is bottomless, husbands hosts, holds all.
Years later it yields them up: whatever I wish
Redeemed from the darkness returns; say then of what matter,
So kitted with cunning, is made my marvellous bag?

THE SECRET

My winter treat, the pantomime at Christmas:
To go out after tea, in frosty dark,
Down by the railway bridge, past the allotments
To the lit hall in the village.
                    I was four.
What was time to me? I thought that Jesus
Lived in the air-raid shelter, I thought that a train
Out of the unmapped dark might bring the Wise Men.
I thought that the whole silent valley brimmed with a secret
That the stars might spell out with their shining.
                    They are gone,
The lit hall, and the laughter; I recall
Nothing of those. Strange then, to see so clearly
That journey down, the glint of moonlit rails,
The frost-furred brick, the snow-capped cabbages,
And all the starry secret, still untold.

RED KITES AT SHIRBURN

Ten years now, since the kites came back to us
Like long-lost aboriginals, restored
To tribal land once theirs, a secret hill,
Wooded, looking west to the clayey plain.
I walk that country; sometimes, trekking across
The green bowl of a valley, eyes cast down,
I sense behind a floating, mid-air, silent,
Anachronistic presence; looking up
I catch the white lilt of a wing, the gleam
Of tawny breast. My step is lighter then.
I spread my hands, not as a falconer
To summon, but to share: show me this land
I am too close to, crop marks under corn,
The dikes of little kingdoms, hangers seamed
With slot and run, the starveling turf's green skin
Taut over ribs of flint, the bald chalk brows
Of silent hills …
            The lift of one long wing
Spills the world sideways, over the wood it goes
Dwindled to a dot; only the call
Comes back to me, like the keen of a ballad singer
Crying lost words, like elf-shot, barbed and bright,
Falling again from immemorial ambush.

ON LEARNING RUSSIAN

Forgive me, I have no rights here.
I am a stranger in this forest
Where the leaves have been falling so long.

Let me wander for a while
Before I address the great trees.
I have a childhood to catch up on

And the paths of language are hard:
Three pairs of iron shoes
I must wear out, before

The witch in the chicken-leg house
Is good to me, before
My quest can be completed

For the well of living water
And the apples that give youth.
Only then, only then may she come,

She that I have sought long,
Who flies from tree to tree:
The fabulous bright falcon,

The phoenix, poetry.

THE BARDS

Not, on the whole, my kind of poetry,
Though poetry can sometimes break from it
Like light from chain-mail. Oh, they had the prowess:
Such mastery as we could never match
Of awdl, englyn, drott-kvaett, lordly measures
Maze-intricate, like loop-stitched tapestries.
They loved to watch the hawk of eloquence
Fly in a bright sky of language. But for what?
Praise of my lord, of my lord's generosity,
A woman's beauty, but she never spoke,
Magnificent laments for noble dead
Thugs and bully-boys. I hear them though,
Voices of scop and skald, of bard and ollamh:
'Say what you like, boy, we were professionals.
The coin of our making bought us more
Than fire and feast: it robed our art with honour.
What poet would not lie to serve such truth?
Our craft was flint and steel, and we struck words
That sparked and kindled, lighting our time's dark,
Though all goes out at last. Can you do more?'

ANOTHER WORLD

Another world, we'd hear the old ones say
When we were small. We were the ones between,
Who followed for a while their closing way,
And saw their footprints fading on the green.

Their rooms were cloud-breath cold when we awoke.
Their bedtime candles lit the cave-dark stair.
Our childhoods hung like threads of chimney-smoke
Suspended in their uneventful air.

They were the last to think that age might come
With reverence, and calm years keeping pace,
And all its end no more than going home
To some unchanging, honourable place.

But they were wrong: swept to one side before
Their dust could fall, irrelevant and strange:
Survivors whom their days outstripped, outwore,
A homespun breed, who saw the fashion change.

They died at last bewildered and alone
And now through us again they truly die
With what they knew, that shall no more be known.
Another world, our children hear us sigh.

REMEMBERING DIDO

They never came back, the young men
Billeted with my grandmother in the Great War
At 40, Church Road, Watford on their way to the Front.
My mother forgot their names, she was only six
And they were too many. One, though, she remembered:
Dido, they called him, who was handsome and merry-hearted,
Who called her Pinky, who teased her about her dolls,
Who tossed her up to the ceiling and caught her again
In strong young cricketer's arms; who died, they heard,
Bullet-riddled, throwing grenades, running forward
Cheering the others on, like a boy at play.
My mother was the last, I think, who knew him,
And she is dead now too. His name was Dido.

AT MARTLESHAM CHURCH

I cannot find the grave I'm looking for
So lay these words instead for tribute: here
My great-grandfather John Finch kept the smithy,
Knowing few things but with great certainty,
His life compressed now to one anecdote
And I the last to have it still by rote:
How toddling at the forge my infant mother,
Back in some burning, bleached Edwardian summer,
Pricked by a horseshoe-nail began to cry,
Was scooped up by strong arms: 'Oh, little chappie!
There there, what's this then – ' trusting watch and chain
To chubby fingers. And if this alone
Endures of all the words he ever said,
I honour now the kindness of the dead.

BY REQUEST

Not lilies, no: I was no gardener.
I spent too many hours in unloved places,
The edge of towns, industrial estates,
Suburban wasteland, shopping precincts, car-parks,
Where the mind must take what cover it can find
In unkempt green, in wayward flowerings
That no-one planned or planted: these were mine.

But do not gather them: let them endure
Wherever they are lodged, in cracks of walls,
By kerb or gutter: plantain, sorrel, dock,
Mugwort and ferny yarrow; if you would
Conjure my ghost, caress again for me
Pineapple-weed's plush yellow eggs; inhale
Some wet dusk, raw with nettle-scent and elder,

Or idly pluck the green darts of wild barley,
Pressing them nib-like on one finger's end
As you stand lost in old hot afternoons.
I shall come, maybe, lighter than the wind
That shakes the castanets of totter grass
And dancing, like the feathered seeds that drift
Sunward, that day the fireweed drops its ash.

APOLOGIA

Because in the bombed city of human existence
There are always too many fires to be put out
   And not enough hands to the pump;

Because I stay myself at a safe distance,
Having no taste for the reek of smoke and sweat
   That is sanctity's true odour;

And because I have seen those who do not flinch
Stagger from the burning, then go back
   To try again, time after time,

I make my apology, and offer instead
This witness that they will not notice, and water
   They will have no time to drink.

AT THE HOSPITAL

The flowers on the sill
Are drooping now, but still
We talk a little, you
Of days we both once knew,
Me watching, till I know
You're tired and I should go.

I put my coat on, stand,
And lightly touch your hand:
'I'll see you then. Take care,'

Then realign my chair
Precisely, to delay
The parting for today.

The young talk love to death.
Not us, we save our breath.
For what is to be said?
The coldness of a bed,
The silence of a room,
A clock that ticks like doom?

No, that is not our way,
But as I go you say
(A gulf, and yet a bridge)
'The yoghurts in the fridge
Need using; don't forget
That card; don't post it yet.'

For this too is love's stuff:
A practical and tough
Care, come day, come night,
To do all things aright,
And all shall be remembered,
I give my parting word.

THE LAST WALK

I am thinking there will have to be a last time
For this evening walk along the quiet lane
To the stile above the sheep-field, where the land
Falls away west, before it starts to climb
To the far line of the downs. I understand.
I only wonder, will it be age and pain
That say 'you will not come this way again'

Or shall I never know it for the last,
That walk I take on some anonymous day
Of grey slow-moving cloud, with hazel leaves
Yellowing in the hedge, the summer past
Yet winter seeming far? If knowing grieves
Then not to know should be the better way.
Perhaps, and yet, I have farewells to say

And seeing all for last, at last may see
The strangeness hidden in familiar ways:
How one short mile, one life, can comprehend
Such weathers, so much love, such memory.
If choice allows then, let me choose the end
That I choose now, and chose so many days,
Walking clear-eyed into the sunset's blaze.

from

UNPUBLISHED POEMS

(2015-2018)

THE LOST LAND

The farmer didn't own it, or he left it,
That corner of the wheatfield, hedged about
With hawthorn, ash and hazel. Here we played,
Lit bonfires in the grass, cooked sausages
Black-skinned and oozing pinkly; made our dens
In hollows of the hedge; on summer evenings
Played oil-drum cricket till the sky grew dark
Then hooted our way home beneath the stars.
We cut and slashed and burned and every year
The land forgave us, gave us blackberries,
Rosehips, hazelnuts, and every year
The butterflies would come, red admirals,
Brimstones, tortoiseshells, quilting the air
With scraps of silk and damask. How we ran
Plucking them like fruit, a dust of scales
Printing our small hot palms, and still the land
Pardoned our savage innocence. We thought,
If we thought at all, it would be there forever
But where can we hide the heart, that time shall not find it?
The tractors cleared the lot one afternoon.
They built a school, and now the mothers come
In four-by-fours to park on tarmacked earth,
Delivering a brood who never guess
What ghosts are here, the lost land, the wild children
Gone with the butterfly summers long ago.

'ONE AFTERNOON OF HEAT
THE EXPRESS-TRAIN ... '

To stand on the railway bridge – that was the dare
When we were children, while the last steam trains
Thundered beneath us, blotting out our world
With acrid gritty grey, and tarry slats
Tingled underfoot. When we came down
Pleased with our childish valour, earth and sky
Unclouding seemed the sweeter: I rejoiced
At sunlight on my face, the song of birds.

Now when I read your poem this comes back
But what I see is not myself but you,
The watchful traveller, nerving yourself
Soon to a more dreadful dare, but then
Getting it down at last, before your world
Was blotted out forever: haycocks, clouds,
While round you, near and far, and farther yet
Than you could ever know, the song went on.

CONSTELLATIONS

We think they never change, but we are wrong.
Our skies were different once: four billion years
Even in the life of stars is long.
See them, by some shifting of time's gears,
Flickering like fairground lights, stars lost
Dulling to cold cinders, stars new-made,
The sky a-glitter like a thawing frost -

So these familiars too, so long arrayed,
Will alter. Yet, while life has eyes to see
One thing's for sure: there will be those who trace
Their time's celestial calligraphy,
Drawing bright legends on the heavens' face
To tame the dark, for this is what we do,
With stories vivid, comforting, untrue.

AFTERLIFE

Suppose that it were true, and when I quit
This body, I become immortal spirit
Let loose to roam among the galaxies
As in an endless forest of glittering trees
With all the worlds to choose and all time yet
To praise and wonder. Shall I then forget
This sojourn in a house of flesh and bone
On a green planet I once called my own?
What if I miss too much this little life,
This company of clouds, trees, children, wife,
Nor find again what flowered in this place
In all the star-filled meadows of deep space?

67P/CHURYUMOV–GERASIMENKO
(Rosetta Space probe, 12/11/2014)

Loner, immemorial wanderer,
You came in from the outer dark and we
Were waiting: now our instrument is lodged,
Nestling like a tick in your dark fur
Of ice and dirt. Misshapen messenger,
Too small for gravity to mould, a duck,
A knobbed potato, lacking all the glamour
Of rings, volcanoes, oceans, who'd have thought
You'd find yourself so singled out, a cosmic
Man in the street, probed for his DNA?
Ah, but what earthly lineage could match
What you, they say, have kept so long and now
May tell at last, the secrets of the Making?

HISTORY

To touch history
Is like dragging the fingertips
Across rough stone.

Wars, famine, plague,
The anonymous misery
Of lightless servitudes
Excoriate.

And to what end
The compassionate, delicate palping
Of poet and annalist?

There is restoration, but what
Restitution? Can the dead inhabit
The houses of our pity?

For knowledge, then: how else
Shall we build for the living?

Also, in gratitude
For the luck of happiness
And days kept safe for us

Like sunlight in the ocean
Of many-layered time
Above that dark abyss.

ENCOUNTER

A rustling by the path in the spring wood.
Stooping, I see a frog, making its way
Through fallen beech leaves under arching brambles,
Hauling itself with splayed elastic limbs
Over dead boughs and bearing as it goes
A froglet, carried pickback like a child.

It stops to look at me, one jewel eye
Pulsing, innocent of past and future,
But in its cells millennia of threat.
The world is web and secret deeper down
Than we can know, and suddenly I cross
A crackling pale brown desert while my heart

Hammers danger danger for what vast
Shadow falls upon me now I freeze
Self-petrifying into yellow stone ...
The moment passes: tall again I stand,
Back off. I wish him well, that traveller
I met in a dry country, far from water.

CENTENARY POEM FOR ROBERT

Hearing your voice on the wireless, I remembered
My youth and your last prime and found the letters
You wrote me long ago, those kind, eccentric
Missives of praise and guidance from a place
I never visited: some magic island
Where you presided in your triple aspect:
Prospero, Ariel and Caliban.

Yet when we met in London you were nothing
But human: white-haired, restless on a couch,
Pained by your back, reviews, and memory.
What did we talk of? Hardy; compost-heaps ...
The house swirled round you, like an undertow.
You blasted my clay poems, or just sometimes
Watched them take wing, and said 'Yes'.

I let you down though: grateful, innocent,
Yet wary, always wary, knowing myself
Unsuitable, meant for no myth but love's
Long ordinariness. I wanted poems
But nothing that went with them: muddle, debts,

The journey, so uncertain, so alone.
You only smiled. 'You will be what you must.

There's no escape, you know.' For you there was
At last, into a twilight, and yet how
To think of you not somewhere, muttering,
Walking under the moon, wholly absorbed,
Knowing yourself beyond conceit a poet,
For me to meet, to share with once again
What we both wanted, poems and nothing else.

ALZHEIMER'S

'Where are you from?' you ask for the seventh time
Since I got here ten minutes ago. I tell you again.
You look at me as you might look at someone
Seen at a distance, looming out of mist.
'I know you, don't I?' Yes, indeed you know me.
I am your brother-in-law, I was four years old
When you came into my life, you brought me comics,
You were full of jokes, you played the clarinet.
Later, you taught me chess: I remember now
The evening that I first beat you, your smiling grace.

I look around: a room, a bed, one chair.
There is a lounge: I found you there when I came
Seated with silent others, watching TV.
Well, they seem kind here, though you cannot go out.
You would wander, lost, they say. As you wander now
By ways I cannot follow, a hunted mind

And all the earths of memory are stopped.
'So, where are you from?', you ask again.

IN MEMORIAM ROY EAGLES

'But Cristes loore and his apostles twelve
He taughte, but first he folwed it hymselve'

We argued once when I was young and still
Argued about such things, you so devout
Trusting in God and Jesus, and me saying
If we want any virtue in this world,
Loving-kindness, courage or compasssion,
We'd better put it there ourselves: that man
Was on his own, God help him. You went on
Preaching, helping, visiting the sick
All your life unswervingly, and I,
What did I do? Wrote poems no one read.

And now I come to stand beside your grave
To tell you what? To make amends, admit
Your make-believe served better than my truth?
Maybe there were angels at your end
And trumpets sounding on the other side,
But what I saw was only human love
Loth to let you go, and bitter loss.
The next life, then, I leave to you: in this one
Grief is a good man's epitaph, and now
In our diminished world we grieve for you.

GRANDSON

That was the first fine day of spring. All day
I split logs in the March sun, and all day
You pottered round, a peaceable companion
Deep in your wordless dream-time, one year old,
Laughing at each 'Hi-ya' as I swung the axe,
But busy with your own endeavours too,
Loading your truck with gravel from the path
To tip it out, chasing the year's first brimstones,
Those scraps of yellow silk, and over and over
Climbing the small hill by the cabbage patch,
To wait each time at the top for my applause.

You won't, of course, remember it, the day
That I remember, this beautiful addition
To set against the slow subtractions of age,
Nor how, the one time I forgot to clap
Your small heroic ascent, you clapped yourself,
King of all castles, beaming expectation,
Confident, as you should be, of this love
That lights my autumn like a new March sun.

WATFORD

'Do you remember Watford?' someone asks
And I am back in nineteen forty-nine,
Getting off the bus, and glad to get off,
Sick from the jolting over Hunton Bridge
And the smell of oil and leather, being met
By a scent of new-ground coffee, and the Pond

With fountains jetting up and lilies floating.
It must have been autumn, I remember the lamps,
The dead leaves damming rain-sluice in the gutter,
The shop-fronts brightly lit, the greasy pavements
Where my shoes made puddling imprints. Tightly I hold
My father's hand through the moving forest of legs.
We are going to Grandma's for tea. A maze of alleys,
A market-place, the golden eyes of haddock
Winking on blue-veined slabs under the lamplight,
A stop for evening paper, cigarettes,
And then a long dark road, and Grandma's house,
Narrow, fronting almost on to the pavement,
A dark hall, and a small blue-aproned woman
Of whom I remember nothing, except she gives me
Boiled eggs on bread-and-butter, and has no toys.
So I sit among the alien conversation
Or pull the curtains back and look out at the night
Coming down dark over apple-trees and fence
And a white path growing dim. Then the goodbye.
'Is he going to see his grandad?' The steep dark stairs
And the bedroom where the old and sick man sits
Propped up on the pillows, in striped pyjamas,
Wheezing a little, and something in the room
Not frightening, but rather to be pitied
If understood, and yet not understood.
'How old is the boy now?' 'I'm five,' I say.
Then out into the night, the rainy darkness,
The moon coming out only once from the billowing clouds,
And the journey back, nose pressed to the rain-pocked window,
My own reflection, floating, hollow-eyed,
On unlit country, blacker than black sky,
Then walking home, across the railway bridge,
Under the seethe of wind-tossed poplar trees,
And stumbling up the path, and into sleep ...
'Watford, you say? That's going back a bit.'

HOMELAND

Flat country is for painters: Norfolk, say,
Its great skies fitted to a perfect rim
Of far-off land, or is it cloud or water?
My country is not like that: here horizons
Lurch from yards to miles: the land is scored
By crease and crumple, rucked to ridge and valley,
But scaled to humans: mountaineers would laugh
At my small hills. Yet always in my dreams
It's these that I come back to: I remember
How once in hospital my wounded spirit
Left my body to heal and went away
Moving like the March wind over the land,
Caressing coombe and covert, lingering
In sunken lanes where violets and stitchwort
Clothe crumbling banks, or by some wooded hanger
Reaching out with ghostly fingertip
To stroke the thin gold foil of beech buds. Young
I loved this country; now as I grow old
I think I am becoming it: my bones
Are chalk and flint, my veins its paths, my skin
Its starveling turf. I match its moods, still dream
That spring will come with blue-white days, though now
Learning like the land to nurse my roots
Through the long pastel quietness of winter.

STOIC

Boys didn't cry, I learnt early
In those bleak years of the Forties
When the ghosts of war still lingered
By wood and field and playground
Wistful for sacrifice,
Lapping the blood of our courage.

And I didn't: gashed knees, heads
Split open by falls from trees,
Stings, burns, arrow-wounds
Elicited no whimper.
I watched as a doctor sewed up
The dangling tip of a finger
Sliced by a spade, then thanked him
For the exercise of his skill.

It was only once, when a girl
Picked me up, motherly,
After some playground tumble
With well-meant words of comfort
That the hot salt shaming tears
Broke through the dam of my courage.
'It's not that bad,' she said.

Oh, but it was, it was.
All hurts I had prepared for
But never the heart-piercing,
Unhealing wounds of kindness.

THE PROPORTIONS OF PITY

Someone I know, out walking with her dog,
Found an abandoned fox-cub; thought it best
At first to leave it, later though came back
To find it still there, shivering and frightened,
So took it to a refuge. That was the day
Nine hundred migrants drowned when their boat capsized
Crossing the Mediterranean. I confess
It was her tale that occupied me more
As if the tug of mere locality
Outweighed all gravity of distant griefs.
Or is it that our pity must be scaled
To what we truly know, to find a place
Within the narrow circle of our kindness?
At least, what came into my dreams that night
Was not drowned children, washed up on a beach,
But only this: a dog's enquiring muzzle
Nuzzling as at a puppy, wanting to play.

ON THE BEACH

That was a good day on the beach at Kynance:
I and my three young sons, building a wall
Between two outcrops where the sea must come,
And all the people joining in, and all
Was summer blaze, was bliss. Our rampart held
A good ten minutes, till the sea reached out
One lazy lion paw and cuffed aside
Sand and stone, a tawny gold-shot tide
That chased us up the beach in laughing rout.

Forty years on, I build another wall,
As age must do, studding the sand of custom
With stones of new endeavour, knowing well
It cannot stay the breaching tide to come
And nothing now is as it was. For look,
The summer crowds have gone, you are alone,
The cliff's cold shadow cutting off the sun,
And on the narrow beach, nowhere to run.
Stoop then, and pick up another stone.

MOMENT

My two small grandsons run ahead of me
Up the coastal path, by grassy banks
Yellow with alexanders, crest a ridge,
Are outlined for a moment, disappear
Into a seablue emptiness of air.

I hurry after, breathless but not yet
A faller by the way, though soon enough
A day must come I cannot bid them wait,
Nor follow through the closing door of air
Into the unmapped years beyond the sky.

And when it comes? Why then, I wish for them
All that I have had: the love of earth,
A serviceable body, friends and one
Much more than friend. And then, in turn, their own
Sweet aftercomers, running on, but first,

Before their vanishing, framed in love's moment.

FRAGMENTS

What are we supposed to do with them
As we grow old, these fragments of memory
That litter the floor of the mind like a broken mirror?

Here I am, six years old,
Standing on the hillside above my home.
Sunlight on red-tiled roofs,
Lines of Monday washing in the back gardens,
A clean soap-scented wind …

From all the blank days, this.

Sometimes it seems to me
There is a task I must do,
That I must piece together
These memories, these moments,
As if each one were a letter,
Like Kay in the Snow Queen's castle,
Trapped here in time, but seeking
The word I must spell out
Which is eternity.

ADONIS BLUE, YOESDEN BANK

Yes, I have loved them, just the way one loves
Unknowingly, until a thing is lost:
Peacocks, tortoisehells, red admirals
Browsing buddleia's sweet purple pastures;
Brimstones, woken by the year's first warmth,
Dancing over bank and brambled ditch;
Once on a beach a fall of painted ladies
Like leaves from some fabulous autumn; orange-tips
And clouded yellows, but never till today
This one, with its wings like summer sky
Bordered with white cloud. It makes the day
Perfect: it distils, it gathers in
The whole of this chalk hillside hazed with flowers,
The hum of sun-warmed grass, the church below
Lost among trees – you'd say that some great artist
Had added to his canvas, Turner-wise,
One drop of purest colour, then stood back
Satisfied at last, his work complete.

SO LONG

Of course, one begins to wonder how it will come
And hopes it will be private: just a discreet
Cough, a tap on the shoulder; one doesn't want
Fuss, a public summons across the water
'Come in, number seven, your time is up.'

One accepts that it is bound to be inconvenient.
There is always so much to do, so much undone.
No chance, I suppose, of persuasion: could you, maybe,
Come back tomorrow, or more formally
'Now I prithee, signieur Death, stand off a while longer'?

Well, I have been trying to put things in order
But really my heart's not in it; selling some books
Is about as far as it's got. There should, of course,
Be messages of love, but I've been trying
Most of my life to send such messages

And the world is busy. So, I think I'll settle
Simply for this: a quiet unheard farewell
And say, for epitaph, that he found being
Difficult, but wouldn't have missed it for worlds.
So long, then, and thanks for all the life.

from

UNPUBLISHED TRANSLATIONS

(2015-2018)

THIS SPOTLESS CHILD
from the French of Jules Supervielle

This spotless child, this rose of chastity,
What's he to do with our carnality?
And was our senses' fury always meant
To find its end in such an innocent?

Henceforth in this new flesh, all turned about,
Shall our love's mystery be acted out?
The passion that once took our hearts by storm
Finds in this cradled guest another form,

In tiny limbs, in little hands, so curled,
In belly, round and innocent of world,
While side by side we watch, for him to tell
Our secret, kept so badly, kept so well.

CE PUR ENFANT

Ce pur enfant, rose de chasteté,
Qu'a-t-il à voir avec la volupté?
Et fallait-il qu'en luxe d'innocence
Allât finir la fureur de nos sens?

Dorénavant en cette neuve chair
Se débattra notre amoureux mystère?
Après nous avoir pris le coeur d'assaut
L'amour se change en l'hôte d'un berceau,

En petits poings fermés, en courtes cuisses,
En ventre rond sans aucune malice
Et nous restons tous deux à regarder
Notre secret si mal, si bien gardé.

A POOR GIRL'S FUNERAL CORTÈGE
from the French of Julien Auguste Pélage Brizeux

When Louise died in her fifteenth year,
A woodland flower, plucked by the wind and rain,
No great procession followed after her:
A single priest, at prayer, led the train.
Behind him came a child, at intervals
Responding to the prayers in muted tone,
Because Louise was poor - even in death
The rich have honours to the poor unknown.
An ancient pall, a boxwood crucifix,
Such were the ornaments of her last bed
And when they came to bear her body off
From its first home to dwell among the dead
Scarcely a mortbell warned the country round
That its most gentle maid was gone away.
Such was her death. But as the convoy went
By furze and leafy copse, at break of day,
Through fields of young green wheat and fragrant vale
April in all its glory was made new:
The coffin of that maiden, as it passed,
Was snowed with blossom, bathed with tears of dew.
A starry bud was trembling on each bough,
The hawthorn, pink and white, was lately dressed.
All was sweet scents and endless harmony
And every bird was singing from its nest.

LE CONVOI D'UNE PAUVRE FILLE

Quand Louise mourut à sa quinzième année,
Fleur des bois par la pluie et le vent moissonnée,
Un cortège nombreux ne suivit pas son deuil:
Un seul prêtre, en priant, conduisait le cercueil;
Puis venait un enfant, qui, d'espace en espace,
Aux saintes oraisons répondait à voix basse;
Car Louise était pauvre, et jusqu'en son trépas
Le riche a des honneurs que le pauvre n'a pas.
La simple croix de buis, un vieux drap mortuaire,
Furent les seuls apprêts de son lit funéraire;
Et quand le fossoyeur, soulevant son beau corps,
Du village natal l'emporta chez les morts,
A peine si la cloche avertit la contrée
Que sa plus douce vierge en était retirée.
Elle mourut ainsi. — Par les taillis couverts,
Les vallons embaumés, les genêts, les blés verts,
Le convoi descendit, au lever de l'aurore.
Avec toute sa pompe avril venait d'éclore,
Et couvrait, en passant, d'une neige de fleurs
Ce cercueil virginal et le baignait de pleurs;
L'aubépine avait pris sa robe rose et blanche,
Un bourgeon étoilé tremblait à chaque branche;
Ce n'étaient que parfums et concerts infinis,
Tous les oiseaux chantaient sur le bord de leurs nids.

CLARA D'ELLÉBEUSE
from the French of Francis Jammes

I loved long ago Clara d'Ellébeuse,
The pupil of old boarding-schools, who came
To sit beneath the lime trees on warm evenings
Reading the magazines of other days.
I love her still, and only her. I feel
The blue light of her white throat on my heart.
Where is she now? Where was that happiness?
Branches would come into her bright room.
Perhaps she is not yet dead, or perhaps we both were.
Dead leaves used to blow about the great courtyard
In the cold wind at the end of long-lost summers.
Do you remember the peacock feathers in the vase
Next to the shells? ... we heard there had been a shipwreck.
They spoke of Newfoundland: The Banks.
Come to me now, Clara d'Ellébeuse.
Let us love each other still, if you still live.
Old tulips may yet bloom in the old garden.
Come quite naked, Clara d'Ellébeuse.

CLARA D'ELLÉBEUSE

J'aime dans le temps Clara d'Ellébeuse,
l'ecolière des anciens pensionnats,
qui allait, les soirs chauds, sous les tilleuls
lire les magazines d'autrefois.
Je n'aime qu'elle, et je sens sur mon coeur
la lumière bleue de sa gorge blanche.
Où est-elle? Où etait donc ce bonheur?
Dans sa chambre claire il entrait des branches.

Elle n'est peut-être pas encore morte
– ou peut-être que nous l'étions tous deux.
La grande cour avait des feuilles mortes
dans le vent froid des fins d'Etés tres vieux.
Te souviens-tu de ces plumes de paon,
dans un grand vase, auprès de coquillages?
On apprenait qu'on avait fait naufrage,
on appelait Terre-Neuve: le Banc.
Viens, viens, ma chère Clara d'Ellébeuse:
aimons-nous encore si tu existes.
Le vieux jardin a de vieilles tulipes.
Viens toute nue, ô Clara d'Ellébeuse.

DEPARTURE
from the German of Heinrich Heine

Now in my breast has died the fire
Of every earthly vain desire,
My hate for wrong has vanished clean,
Likewise as if it had not been
Care for my own and others' ill.
Now only death lives in me still.

The curtain falls, the play is done,
And my dear German public's gone
Yawning on their way back home.
Those little folk are not so dumb:
They'll eat, drink, laugh and sing tonight,
And take full pleasure. He was right,
That noble hero, he who said
In Homer's book, as I once read,

The meanest Philistine alive
In Stuttgart town may better thrive
Than I, Achilles, in this bed,
A prince of shades among the dead.

DER SCHEIDENDE

Erstorben ist in meiner Brust
Jedwede weltlich eitle Lust,
Schier is mir auch erstorben drin
Der Hass des Schlechten, sogar der Sinn
Für eigne wie für fremde Not –
Und in mir lebt noch nur der Tod!

Der Vorhang fällt, das Stück ist aus,
Und gähnend wandelt jetzt nach Haus
Mein liebes deutsches Publikum,
Die guten Leutchen sind nicht dumm;
Das speist jetzt ganz vergnügt zu Nacht,
Und trinkt sein Schöppchen, singt und lacht –
Er hatte recht, der edle Heros,
Der weiland sprach im Buch Homeros':
Der kleinste lebendige Philister
Zu Stukkert am Neckar, viel glücklicher ist er
Als ich, der Pelide, der tote Held,
Der Schattenfürst in der Unterwelt.

MORPHINE
from the German of Heinrich Heine

How alike they are, two beautiful
Forms of young men, though at the same time one
Much paler than the other, more severe,
I might even say, much more distinguished-looking
Than this, the other, who took me in his arms
So trustingly. How soft his smile, how loving
That gaze of his. Almost one might say
That poppy-wreath he wears around his head
Touched my own temples too, and drove out pain
With that strange scent it brings. But such relief
Lasts little time: now I can be quite well
Only when the other dips his torch,
The older brother, serious and pale.
Sleep is good, death better, but indeed
The best of all, never to have been born.

MORPHINE

Gross ist die Ähnlichkeit der beiden schönen
Jünglingsgestalten, ob der eine gleich
Viel blässer als der andre, auch viel strenger,
Fast möchte ich sagen viel vornehmer aussieht
Als jener andre, welcher mich vertraulich
In seine Arme schloss – Wie lieblich sanft
War dann sein Lächeln, und sein Blick wie selig!
Dann mocht es wohl geschehn, dass seines Hauptes
Mohnblumenkranz auch meine Stirn berührte
Und seltsam duftend allen Schmerz verscheuchte
Aus meiner Seel – Doch solche Linderung,

Sie dauert kurze Zeit; genesen gänzlich
Kann ich nur dann, wenn seine Fackel senkt
Der andre Bruder, der so ernst und bleich. –
Gut ist der Schlaf, der Tod ist besser – freilich
Das beste wäre, nie geboren sein.

MY DAY WAS HAPPY
from the German of Heinrich Heine

My day was happy, fortunate my night,
My people praised me when I struck the lyre.
My poet's art was passion; by its fire
Many a heart was kindled to delight.

My summer days bloom on, but now my crop
Is in the barn; the time has come to leave
All that I have loved so well and grieve
That what the world made dear to me must stop.

My hand sinks from the strings and plays no more,
The glass is shattered I would raise before
To my too trusting lips so gladly pressed.

O God! how loath a thing it is to die,
How sweet to live and see the days go by
Safe in the earth's familiar sweet nest.

MEIN TAG WAR HEITER

Mein Tag war heiter, glücklich meine Nacht.
Mir jauchzte stets mein Volk, wenn ich die Leier
Der Dichtkunst schlug. Mein Lied war Lust und Feuer,
Hat manche schöne Gluten angefacht.
Noch blüht mein Sommer, dennoch eingebracht
Hab ich die Ernte schon in meine Scheuer –
Und jetzt soll ich verlassen, was so teuer,
So lieb und teuer mir die Welt gemacht!
Der Hand entsinkt das Saitenspiel. In Scherben
Zerbricht das Glas, das ich so fröhlich eben
An meine übermütgen Lippen preßte.
O Gott! wie häßlich bitter ist das Sterben!
O Gott! wie süß und traulich läßt sich leben
In diesem traulich süßen Erdenneste!

GUDRUN'S LAMENT
from the Old Norse poem Guðrúnarkviða

My Sigurd stood above the sons of Gjuki
As the tall spear-leek stands above the grass
Or the long-legged hart above the lesser beasts
Or the red gold above grey silver
Or as if he were the bright stone on a bracelet,
The arkenstone, precious among princes.
And I myself seemed to the leader of men
A maid of Odin's hosts, higher than any.
Now I am nothing, like a leafless tree
Laid low by my king's death, at board and bed
Missing my good gossip …

Svá var minn Sigurðr hjá sonum Gjúka
sem væri geirlaukr ór grasi vaxinn,
eða hjörtr hábeinn um hvössum dyrum,
eða gull glód-rautt af grá silfri,
eða væri bjartr steinn á band dreginn,
jarknasteinn yfir öðlingum.
Ek þótta ok þjóðans rekkum
hverri hæri Herjans dísi;
nú em ek svá lítil sem lauf séi
oft í jölstrum at jöfur dauðan.
Sakna ek i sessa ok i saeingu
Mins málvinar …

AUTUMN DAY
from the German of Rainer Maria Rilke

Lord, it is time. The great summer is done.
Let loose the winds upon the meadows, let
Your shadows count the last hours of the sun.
Bid the late fruits to swell upon the vine,
Allow them two more days of southern heat,
Cram the last ripeness into them, complete
Their sweet fulfilment in full-bodied wine.
Who has no house now shall not make a home
Again; who is alone now long shall be so,
Will sit up, read, will write long letters, go
Along the avenues, restless to roam
While the leaves keep drifting, to and fro.

HERBSTTAG

Herr, es ist Zeit. Der Sommer war sehr groß.
Leg deinen Schatten auf die Sonnenuhren,
und auf den Fluren laß die Winde los.

Befiehl den letzten Früchten voll zu sein;
gib ihnen noch zwei südliche Tage,
dränge sie zur Vollendung hin, und jage
die letzte Süße in den schweren Wein.

Wer jetzt kein Haus hat, baut sich keines mehr.
Wer jetzt allein ist, wird es lange bleiben,
wird wachen, lesen, lange Briefe schreiben
und wird in den Alleen hin und her
unruhig wandern, wenn die Blätter treiben.

'FROM HER EARLIEST YEARS…'
from the French of Victor Hugo

From her earliest years, this was her thing
To come into my room a while each morning.
I'd wait, as for a sunbeam to appear.
She'd march in, say 'Good morning, little father,'
Sit down on my bed, take up my pen,
Open my books, muddle my papers, laughing,
Then like a bird of passage she'd be gone
And I, with clearer head, begin again
My interrupted work, often to find
Some zany arabesque she'd left behind

Among my manuscripts, a sketch she'd traced,
And then, blank pages that her hands had creased.
Somehow, my best lines fell between those folds.
She loved God, flowers, starry skies, green fields.
Before she was a woman, she was spirit
And from her clear eyes her bright soul shone out.
She quizzed me constantly, upon all things.
Ah, but the warm glow of those winter evenings
When we'd talk language, grammar, history,
Their mother near, four children at my knee,
A few friends by the hearth and much to say –
That was a life to which content came easy.
And now to think that she is dead! God help me,
For I, when she was sad, was never happy.
I took no joy in joyous balls and parties
If parting I'd seen shadow in her eyes.

'ELLE AVAIT PRIS CE PLI ... '

Elle avait pris ce pli dans son âge enfantin
De venir dans ma chambre un peu chaque matin;
Je l'attendais ainsi qu'un rayon qu'on espère;
Elle entrait, et disait: Bonjour, mon petit père;
Prenait ma plume, ouvrait mes livres, s'asseyait
Sur mon lit, dérangeait mes papiers, et riait,
Puis soudain s'en allait comme un oiseau qui passe.
Alors, je reprenais, la tête un peu moins lasse,
Mon oeuvre interrompue, et, tout en écrivant,
Parmi mes manuscrits je rencontrais souvent
Quelque arabesque folle et qu'elle avait tracée,
Et mainte page blanche entre ses mains froissée
Où, je ne sais comment, venaient mes plus doux vers.

Elle aimait Dieu, les fleurs, les astres, les prés verts,
Et c'était un esprit avant d'être une femme.
Son regard reflétait la clarté de son âme.
Elle me consultait sur tout à tous moments.
Oh! que de soirs d'hiver radieux et charmants
Passés à raisonner langue, histoire et grammaire,
Mes quatre enfants groupés sur mes genoux, leur mère
Tout près, quelques amis causant au coin du feu!
J'appelais cette vie être content de peu!
Et dire qu'elle est morte! Hélas! que Dieu m'assiste!
Je n'étais jamais gai quand je la sentais triste;
J'étais morne au milieu du bal le plus joyeux
Si j'avais, en partant, vu quelque ombre en ses yeux.

THE SWAN
from the Old English of the Exeter Book

My garb is silent when I go on earth
Where men abide, or when I stir the stream
Sometimes, though, I harness the high air,
Men's dwellings dwindle as I mount above
Borne on the mighty sky. What music then
My rustling raiment makes, what melodies
It sings in splendour as I soar aloft,
A faring spirit far from field and flood.

Hrægl min swigað   þôn ic hrusan trede
oþþe þa wic buge   oþþe wado drefe
hwilum mec ahebbað   ofer hæleþa byht
hyrste mine   þeos hea lyft

mec þôn wide   wolcna strengu
ofer folc byreð   frætwe mine
swogað hlude   swinsiað
torhte singað   þôn ic getenge ne beom
flode ond foldan   ferende gæst

SONG 8
from the Latin of Gaius Valerius Catullus

Catullus, you poor fool, stop faffing about
And face the facts: she's gone, the one you loved
More than any girl will ever be loved.
How bright the sun shone for you once, when she
Would lead and you would follow her whenever
Even to that place of many pleasures
That you desired, and she did not deny.
Indeed, the sun shone brightly for you then
And now, she does not want you. So, you too,
Left with no other power, learn not to want:
Don't follow one who runs away, don't live
A lovesick fool: man up, man, and endure.
Goodbye then, girl – Catullus is enduring –
He will not miss you, will not ask for you
Since you are loth. Let it be your turn, bitch,
To grieve when none desire you. For who now
Will come to you and call you beautiful?
Whom will you love? Whose will they say you are?
Whom will you kiss? What lips now will you nibble?
Only, Catullus, stay strong and endure.

CARMEN 8

Miser Catulle, desinas ineptire,
et quod vides perisse perditum ducas.
Fulsere quondam candidi tibi soles,
cum ventitabas quo puella ducebat
amata nobis quantum amabitur nulla.
Ibi illa multa cum iocosa fiebant,
quae tu volebas nec puella nolebat,
fulsere vere candidi tibi soles.
Nunc iam illa non vult: tu quoque impotens noli,
nec quae fugit sectare, nec miser vive,
sed obstinata mente perfer, obdura.
Vale puella, iam Catullus obdurat,
nec te requiret nec rogabit invitam.
At tu dolebis, cum rogaberis nulla.
Scelesta, vae te, quae tibi manet vita?
Quis nunc te adibit? cui videberis bella?
Quem nunc amabis? Cuius esse diceris?
Quem basiabis? Cui labella mordebis?
At tu, Catulle, destinatus obdura.

GOING BLIND
from the German of Rainer Maria Rilke

She sat just like the rest of them at tea.
What struck me first was how she held her cup
Not quite the same as others in the group.
She sometimes smiled. It almost hurt to see.

And when the others rose at last and went
From room to room, taking their random way,
Laughing and talking, with so much to say,
I saw her. She was following, intent

On some thought of her own, like one aware
She soon would have to sing for many people,
While light on her bright eyes, as on a pool,
Gleamed from beyond, reflecting gladness there.

She followed slowly, so long passing by
As if there were still something to surmount;
And yet, once she had mastered that ascent,
She would no more be walking, but would fly.

DIE ERBLINDENDE

Sie saß so wie die anderen beim Tee.
Mir war zuerst, als ob sie ihre Tasse
ein wenig anders als die andern fasse.
Sie lächelte einmal. Es tat fast weh.

Und als man schließlich sich erhob und sprach
und langsam und wie es der Zufall brachte
durch viele Zimmer ging (man sprach und lachte),
da sah ich sie. Sie ging den andern nach,

verhalten, so wie eine, welche gleich
wird singen müssen und vor vielen Leuten;
auf ihren hellen Augen die sich freuten
war Licht von außen wie auf einem Teich.

Sie folgte langsam und sie brauchte lang
als wäre etwas noch nicht überstiegen;
und doch: als ob, nach einem Übergang,
sie nich mehr gehen würde, sondern fliegen.

A YEAR HAS PASSED
from the Norwegian of Arnulf Øverland

A year has passed, Beate,
That you know nothing of.
I watch a sunless summer wane.
Beate, autumn's come again.
I stand here by your grave.

How quiet it must be, that night,
When all that happens is no more,
With nothing to remember now
Nor memory of things before.

How glad you would have been to live,
But in the dark your soul was shut.
God wandered over land and sea
And as he went quite casually
He trod you underfoot.

A year has passed, Beate.
Onwards it streams, time's golden sea,
That granted you too little life
And left too much for me.

ET ÅR ER GÅTT

Et år er gått, Beate,
Det vet du ikke av.
Der gikk en solløs sommer hen.
Beate, det er høst igjen.
Her står jeg ved din grav.

Hvor tyst må natten vaere
der intet mere finnes,
og når vi ikke minnes
og intet minnes mere.

Du vilde gjerne leve,
men mørket favner om din sjel.
Gud vandret over jorden
Og helt tilfeldig trådte
Han på dig med sin hæl.

Et år er gått, Beate.
Det strømmer, tidens golde hav.
Det liv du fikk forlate,
Fikk jeg for meget av.

MY BROTHER WAS A PILOT
from the German of Bertolt Brecht

My brother was a pilot
His papers came one day
He got his kit together
And took a southward way.

My brother is a conqueror
Our people need more space
And winning territory by war's
An old dream of our race.

The space in the Spanish mountains
My brother got to keep
Measures just six feet in length
And is five foot deep.

MEIN BRUDER WAR EIN FLIEGER

Mein Bruder war ein Flieger
Eines Tages bekam er eine Kart
Er hat seine Kiste eingepackt
Und südwärts ging die Fahrt.

Mein Bruder ist ein Eroberer
Unserm Volke fehlt's an Raum
Und Grund und Boden zu kriegen, ist
Bei uns alter Traum.

Der Raum, den mein Bruder eroberte
Liegt im Guadarramamassiv
Er ist lang einen Meter achtzig
Und einen Meter fünfzig tief.

THE FOX
from the Welsh of R Williams Parry

Just as we neared the summit, when below
The Sabbath bells were calling all to service
And when a July sun's unstinted glow
Was calling to the mountain – in that place
He came, unwary, on quiet feet, alone
In his rare beauty. And the three of us
Stood there, transfixed, a trinity in stone,
And he too, frozen in mid-step, his eyes
Above one poised foot like twin flames, quite still,
Watching us. And so, just for that moment,
We stood, and did not move or breathe, until
Unhurriedly and without fear he went
And it was done: beyond the ridge red fur
Flashed for an instant, like a falling star.

Y LLWYNOG

Ganllath o gopa'r mynydd, pan oedd clych
Eglwysi'r llethrau'n gwahodd tua'r llan,
Ac anrheuliedig haul Gorffennaf gwych
Yn gwahodd tua'r mynydd – yn y fan,
Ar ddiarwybod droed a distaw duth,
Llwybreiddiodd ei ryfeddod prin o'n blaen
Ninnau heb ysgog ac heb ynom chwyth
Barlyswyd ennyd; megis trindod faen
Y safem, pan ar ganol diofal gam
Syfrdan y safodd yntau, ac uwchlaw
Ei untroed oediog dwy sefydlog fflam
Ei lygaid arnom. Yna heb frys na braw
Llithrodd ei flewyn cringoch dros y grib;
Digwyddodd, darfu, megis seren wîb.

INDEX OF TITLES

67P/Churyumov–Gerasimenko 232

A Candle for Mr Sokolowski 186

A Local History 95

A Poor Girl's Funeral Cortège 250

A Year Has Passed 265

Absences 68

Acceptance 202

Accidentals 154

Adonis Blue, Yoesden Bank 244

Afterlife 231

Against Geologies 131

Alzheimer's 235

Amnio 159

Anniversary 107

Another Small Incident 101

Another World 220

Apologia 223

Appeals 72

At Martlesham Church 221

At Steep 196

At The Funeral 137

At The Hospital 223

At the Open-air Market 78

Audit 108

Autumn Day 258

Barna-Oddr 141

Beth's Room 130

Beyond 189

Birds at Pagham 96

Blackbird at Dusk, February 84

Blackthorn Day 204

Blooding 93

By Request 222

Centenary Poem for Robert 234

Chiltern Country 62

Clara d'Ellébeuse 252

Climbing to the Ridge 148

Compromise 213

Consider 156

Constellations 230

Cool Medium 69

Cosmologies 190

CV 178

Daughter, Aged Five *160*

December Love *44*

Departure *253*

Division *27*

Dolphin-watching *175*

Doppelganger *146*

Dune Country *104*

Earth to Earth *162*

Earthworms *56*

Embassy *187*

Encounter *233*

Endangered Species *167*

Envoi *146*

Estate *40*

Evening after Rain *42*

Expanding Universe *208*

Farewell to the Classics *73*

Father *64*

Finders Keepers *109*

First Night *203*

Flints *77*

For Beth *116*

Fragments *243*

Frogs *84*

From her earliest years *259*

From The Train *139*

Gaia's Dream *97*

Game's End *47*

Geomancies *140*

Going Blind *263*

Grandson *237*

Gudrun's Lament *257*

Haiku for a Lunar Eclipse *125*

Harvest *79*

Heatwave *145*

Hedge *144*

Heroic Ideal *188*

History *232*

Homeland *239*

Hush-a-bye, Baby *133*

Immigrants *191*

In Memoriam Roy Eagles *236*

In Memory of Edward Thomas, 1878-1917 *71*

In The Playground *119*

In The Staff-Room *35*

January Morning *210*

January Night *158*

Journal *189*

Lament of the Old Woman of Beare *33*

Language *212*

Leap Second (31/12/2008) *208*

Lessons *81*

Limestone Pavement *167*

Logos *211*

Lost *108*

Love after the Fall *46*

Lucre *165*

Map-maker *113*

Marathon Man *102*

May Day *85*

Meetings *91*

Miranda *46*

Moment *242*

Morphine *255*

Mother *66*

Museum Piece *173*

My Brother was a Pilot *266*

My Day Was Happy *256*

My People *134*

Naming The Moths *141*

Newborn *65*

Night *115*

Njal *170*

No Answer *161*

No Other Elegy *31*

No Through Road *201*

Not Daffodils *99*

Not to be Born *61*

Novices *182*

October Fungi *106*

Odd *67*

On a Book of Nature
    Photography *88*

On Learning Russian *218*

On The Beach *241*

On The Motorway *121*

Once Upon A Time *152*

One afternoon of heat the
    express-train *230*

One Country *181*

Out on a Limb *23*

Outskirts *102*

Parents *205*

Paths *127*

Pen-friend *143*

Place-names *120*

Plural *131*

Postcard from Pembrokeshire
    90

Pregnant *39*

Prognosis *134*

Raggle Taggle *210*

Reading Icelandic Sagas *70*

Red Kites At Shirburn *217*

Rejects *176*

Relatively Speaking *123*

Remembering Dido *221*

Remembering The Picnic *177*

Retirement *180*

Returning after Absence *56*

Riddle *216*

Rooms *207*

RTFP *204*

Say *92*

Scents *114*

Seaside Honeymoon *25*

Second Summer *135*

Settlements *117*

She *147*

Silva *215*

Sixty *190*

Sleep *66*

Slide Show *209*

Small Incident in Library *83*

So Long *244*

So Soon *214*

Something Else *104*

Song 8 *262*

Squirrel *94*

Starlings *43*

Stellar Sequence *103*

Stoic *240*

Stroke Case *31*

Student's Window, Bath
   University *62*

Success *164*

Summer Rain *33*

Survivor *129*

Taxonomical Note *68*

The Anger of the Loving *122*

The Bards *219*

The Beech Tree *136*

The Beechwoods, Autumn *105*

The Birds *174*

The Birth of Poems *173*

The Bonfire *48*

The Cherry Tree *155*

The Computer Room,
   Midnight *80*

The Craft *202*

The Craftsmen *192*

The Disused Well *70*

The Dreamers *138*

The Flowers *30*

The Fox *268*

The Good Old Days *169*

The Good Words *172*

The Haunted Road *98*

The Hillside *82*

The House *193*

The House Martins *91*

The Lame Ant *151*

The Last Walk *225*

The Lost Land *229*

The Lost Weathers *168*

The Maharajah's Well *126*

The Nestlings *38*

The Planet Happiness *177*

The Programmer's Tale *185*

The Proportions of Pity *241*

The Puzzle *132*

The Refusal *179*

The Remembrance (May 8, 1995) *156*

The Ripples *32*

The Secret *216*

The Sleeper *166*

The Solution *44*

The Strangeness *55*

The Summer Country *153*

The Swan *261*

The Tree of Frost *29*

The Unforgiven *212*

The Visit *87*

The Visitors *161*

The Wave *63*

The Woods *194*

This Spotless Child *249*

Three for Runners *89*

To Air *195*

Two Trees *28*

Underwater *57*

Urban Grass *128*

Valediction *98*

Virtual Reality *206*

Vocabularies *124*

Water Music *74*

Watford *237*

Wedding Dress *27*

Widow *118*

Winter Wood *77*

Yobs *86*

GREENWICH EXCHANGE SELECTED POETRY LIST

Gary ALLEN
Jackson's Corner
£11.99 (pbk) ♦ 94pp ♦ 2016
978-1-910996-03-4

Joseph ALLEN
Clabber Street Blues
£11.99 (pbk) ♦ 88pp ♦ 2016
978-1-910996-07-2

Charles BAUDELAIRE
Fleurs de Mal (edited F.W. Leakey)
£9.95 (pbk) ♦ 160pp ♦ 1997
978-1-871551-10-5

Maggie BUTT
Lipstick
£7.99 (pbk) ♦ 72pp ♦ 2007
978-1-871551-94-5

Michael CULLUP
A Change of Season
£9.95 (pbk) ♦ 98pp ♦ 2010
978-1-906075-38-5

Michael CULLUP
Matelot
£11.99 (pbk) ♦ 132pp ♦ 2016
978-1-906075-95-8

Simon DAVID
a rainbow of only one hue
£11.95 (pbk) ♦ 96pp ♦ 2016
978-1-910996-99-7

John GREENING
Hunts: Poems 1979-2009
£7.99 (pbk) ♦ 262 pp ♦ 2009
978-1-906075-33-0

Sean HALDANE
The Memory Tree
£9.99 (pbk) ♦ 90pp ♦ 2015
978-1-906075-94-1

Sean HALDANE
Always Two: Poems 1966-2009
£15.99 (pbk) ♦ 268pp ♦ 2009
978-1-906075-22-4

Ralph HODGSON
The Last Blackbird & Other Poems
£7.95 (pbk) ♦ 68pp ♦ 2004
978-1-871551-81-5

Warren HOPE
First Light & Other Poems
£9.99 (pbk) ♦ 60pp ♦ 2013
978-1-906075-80-4

Warren HOPE
Adam's Thoughts in Winter
£4.99 (pbk) ♦ 46pp ♦ 2001
978-1-871551-40-2

Gordon JARVIE
A Man Passing Through
£16.99 (pbk) ♦ 252pp ♦ 2014
978-1-906075-89-7

Gordon JARVIE
Endgame
£11.99 (pbk) ♦ 80pp ♦ 2016
978-1-910996-98-0

John LUCAS
Portable Property
£9.99 (pbk) ♦ 82pp ♦ 2015
978-1-910996-00-3

Hollie MCNISH
Papers
£11.95 (pbk) ♦ 76pp ♦ 2012
978-1-906075-67-5

Derwent MAY
Wondering About Many Women
£7.99 (pbk) ♦ 46pp ♦ 2011
978-1-906075-62-0

Robert NYE
An Almost Dancer
£7.99 (pbk) ♦ 58pp ♦ 2012
978-1-906075-39-2

Robert NYE
The Rain and the Glass
£6.99 (pbk) ♦132pp ♦ 2004
978-1-871551-41-9

Steven O'BRIEN
Scrying Stone
£7.99 (pbk) ♦ 70pp ♦ 2010
978-1-906075-56-9

Marnie POMEROY
Blue Moon
£9.99 (pbk) ♦ 76pp ♦ 2015
978-1-910996-02-7

Marnie POMEROY
The Flaming
£7.99 (pbk) ♦ 80pp ♦ 2010
978-1-906075-43-9

Martin SEYMOUR-SMITH
Collected Poems 1943-1993
£9.99 (pbk) ♦ 184pp ♦ 2006
978-1-871551-47-1

Martin SEYMOUR-SMITH
Wilderness
£4.99 (pbk) ♦ 52pp ♦ 1994
978-1-871551-08-2

David SUTTON
No Through Road
£9.99 (pbk) ♦ 48pp ♦ 2013
978-1-906075-77-4

Jim C. WILSON
Come Close and Listen
£9.99 (pbk) ♦ 88pp ♦ 2014
978-1-906075-85-9

Stephen WILSON
Fluttering Hands
£7.95 (pbk) ♦ 80pp ♦ 2008
978-1-906075-19-4